Practical Partnership Agreements

Practical Partnership Agreements

Tony Sacker
Partner, Kingsley Napley, London

jORDANS

1995

Published by
Jordan Publishing Limited
21 St Thomas Street
Bristol BS1 6JS

British Library Cataloguing-in-Publication Data
A catalogue record for this book is available from the British Library.

ISBN 0 85308 212 X

Typeset by Interactive Sciences, Gloucester
Printed in Great Britain by Bookcraft (Bath) Ltd, Midsomer Norton

PREFACE

This is a book of precedent agreements and forms relevant to partnerships, written for professionals (not only solicitors) who advise existing and prospective partners about their businesses. As an introduction to the agreements themselves, I offer some drafting tips which I have found useful, and reminders about the legal principles which underpin all partnerships.

Since a partnership is a contract of good faith between individuals in business, trust and mutual reliance are the keystones of the relationship. Therefore, I give the following advice to each of my clients who is considering partnership.

'Ask yourself the following questions in the following order:

Do you *like* your prospective partners?
If yes, do you *trust* them?
If you do, are they *competent*?
If they are, does the *financial proposal* seem worthwhile?

If the answer to any question is 'no' then do not proceed to the next question – just don't go into the partnership.'

Partnership is the most flexible form of business arrangement available in England and Wales. No formality is required for the formation of a partnership, and such informality can give rise to potentially serious and sometimes terminal problems for a firm. A properly drafted agreement is essential if a firm is not to be prejudiced by lack of forethought.

No business can survive without its customers. They do not want the firm to have internal problems and if the firm's problems do become apparent, those customers of the firm will take their business elsewhere. The object of this book, then, is to avoid disputes by applying forethought at the outset, and by doing so to provide for a successful business.

Writing a book, whilst heading a busy commercial department in a firm of solicitors, is a major undertaking. My partners at Kingsley Napley have given especial help (our agreement takes account of authorship!) in enabling me to make the time and effort to write this book. Particular acknowledgement is due to my tax partner, Marc Selby, for his contribution to the taxation aspects, as well as for having his ear bent on many occasions on matters of principle and drafting. My wife, Frances, has given me tremendous support and encouragement as well as tolerating innumerable wrecked weekends, paper everywhere, and lack of access to our word processor. Martin West of Jordans, who conceived the idea of this book, has encouraged, jollied and threatened me until together we have brought it to publication. To all of them I express my grateful, heartfelt thanks and appreciation.

Tony Sacker
August 1995

CONTENTS

Note: The precedents contained in this book are also available on disk. For further details and an order form, please contact our customer services department:

Jordan Publishing Limited
21 St Thomas Street
Bristol BS1 6JS
tel: 0117 923 0600
fax: 0117 925 0486

INTRODUCTION

This introduction is arranged under the following topic headings:

ABOUT THIS BOOK AND PARTNERSHIP

Partnership is the common form of business arrangement for professionals in England and Wales. Accordingly, this book concentrates on precedents of agreements for professional firms (eg solicitors, accountants and surveyors) for whom the culture of partnership is a normal part of their everyday working lives.

For most trading enterprises, a private limited company is a more suitable business vehicle; the exposure to joint and several liability plus the adverse effect on the business of a planned (or unplanned) dissolution mean that there are relatively few circumstances in which an experienced practitioner would recommend partnership to non-family trading enterprises. However, I have included a trading partnership agreement for those smaller businesses, usually of a family nature, which prefer not to incorporate.

Husband and wife partnerships are often created for taxation rather than commercial reasons – the Two Partners precedent will form a useful basis, but practitioners should be aware of the dual risks involved. First, the Inland Revenue will not accept the arrangement if it is a sham; secondly, if there is a divorce, a successful business could be exposed to winding-up at the same time as the marriage.

Partnership is about relationships between individuals, not about commercial arrangements between organisations. It imposes on partners obligations of openness and fair dealing with one another. The relationship between partners, like a good marriage, depends upon give and take. Moreover, it combines in each partner, three areas of responsibility which are separated in the corporate structure, namely ownership, management and work. These are issues of which the draftsman must be aware.

For some of us, our professional code does not permit incorporation (or, even if it permits incorporation, it does not permit limitation of liability), but even without such professional constraint the ethos and culture of our businesses would not be very different. After all, the traditional definition of a profession, to which we still subscribe, is of a calling in which the interests of the clients or customers of the business are put before those of the business itself. The provision of a service to clients creates an atmosphere within the professional firm of collegiality for which the partnership is the natural business vehicle.

The precedents in this book are not designed for management structures and profit variation provisions appropriate to large firms (say 20 plus partners); nor do they cover nominee companies for property holdings or the provisions of the Limited Partnerships Act 1907.

ABOUT THE PRECEDENTS

Flexibility – Loose-leaf Agreements

Section 19 of the Partnership Act 1890 states:

> 'The mutual rights and duties of partners, whether ascertained by agreement or defined by this Act, may be varied by the consent of all the partners, and such consent may be either express or inferred from a course of dealing.'

This short section of the statute gives an exceptional degree of flexibility to partnership arrangements. As lawyers will understand, it is only rarely (other than in partnerships) that an agreement made by a deed can be varied verbally or by informal written documents. The effect of section 19 is that a 'loose-leaf' partnership agreement becomes a practical and legal format. All of the Partnership Agreements in this book are intended to be used as loose-leaf documents and are drafted with that in mind.

The advantages of the loose-leaf format are immediately apparent. Deeds of Admission of New Partners and Deeds of Retirement become unnecessary because the Agreements themselves cope with these eventualities. A partner can be admitted merely by signing the existing Agreement. Variations are dealt with by inserting replacement pages in the Agreement, rather than Deeds of Variation. However, I do include an outline form of Deed of Admission and Deed of Retirement for those situations where the principal Agreement is not in the loose-leaf format.

Drafting Style

Partnership Agreements are working documents and I have therefore adopted a drafting style to suit such documents.

When drafting complicated documents, the draftsman has a number of different options of style. Two contrasting styles are textbook and reference book style. A textbook is written to be read from beginning to end. It expounds its subject in a logical way starting with simple statements of principle at the beginning and developing the topic serially from there. A reference book is not designed in this way.

It is a book for those with a basic understanding of the topic who wish to find an answer to one or more questions quickly and clearly. The key to such a book is an effective index which leads the reader rapidly to the particular topic in which he or she is interested. Once the topic is found it will, of course, normally be written in a textbook style.

A Partnership Agreement is a work of reference. It is not a novel to be read from beginning to end, so I have adopted a reference-book style of layout and indexing.

The agreement itself deals with various discrete aspects of the partnership affairs and falls naturally into separate sections which are best dealt with by individual Schedules. Thus, the Standard Form Agreement is divided into the following sections:

Principal Clauses:

Establishment of the firm, changes of partners, and partners' mutual duties.

Schedules:

Dissolution

Financial

Interpretation

Meetings and voting

Partners list

Repayments to partners who leave or die

Termination and suspension

EXecution

Each Schedule is identified by letter rather than number – the letter indicating the nature of the contents of the Schedule. Thus, Schedule **D** contains provisions relating to **D**issolution. Clauses within Schedules are numbered so as to identify them with the particular Schedule in which they are contained. Thus, the first Clause in Schedule D is Clause D1. Consequently, at any point in the Agreement the reader is aware of the Schedule in which a Clause is contained without turning backwards and forwards and the topic to which the Schedule relates. References to other Clauses can be expressed in briefer terms, so that instead of referring to 'Clause 1 in Schedule D' one can simply refer to 'Clause D1'.

All of the interpretation and definition Clauses are contained in a separate Schedule (Schedule **I** **I**nterpretation). If the document is produced in a loose-leaf format, it is possible for a reader to extract that Schedule from the binder and therefore to have both the definitions and the text open at the same time, again avoiding continual turning of pages. A first-time reader of the document would be well advised to read Schedule **I** before any other part of the document.

Defined terms are identified in the precedents by capitalisation. Two particular areas where Partnership Agreements change on a frequent basis are further identified, namely, shares in the firm and voting percentages. Profit and capital shares and drawings percentages are in Table **F** at the end of Schedule **F** (**F**inancial) so that changes in profit shares and the admission and departure of partners can easily be incorporated into the document without major amendment. Similarly, as to voting, the Agreements use throughout as defined terms 'Resolution' or 'Resolve' when referring to partners' decisions. The relevant percentages for each type of Resolution are then set out in Table **M** at the end of Schedule **M** (**M**eetings). This enables Partners to change the voting balance as a firm grows in size (see Management and Decision-making in 'About Drafting Agreements').

ABOUT THE LAW

This topic is divided into the following sub headings:

The Partnership Act 1890 and other relevant statutes appear in the Appendix at the rear of the book.

Introduction

Partnership law has evolved over the centuries since Roman times. It is characterised by three principal themes.

The first theme is that a Partnership Agreement is a *contract* into which the law may imply certain terms (almost all of which can be negated by the partners). The law also imposes certain obligations in relation to third parties most of which can be excluded only by express agreement with the third party.

The second theme is an obligation of *good faith* between the partners. This is demonstrated by the following clause which is implied into every Agreement:

> 'A partner shall be just and faithful in all his or her dealings with the Partnership Business and will give a true and full account of all his or her dealings with the Partnership Business whenever called upon to do so by another Partner.'

The obligations expressed in this clause are so fundamental to the nature of partnership that if they were negated or excluded, the arrangement between the parties would cease to be a partnership at all.

The third theme is found in the Partnership Act 1890 which provides that:

Section 1(1):
> 'Partnership is the relation which subsists between persons carrying on a business in common with a view to profit.'

In other words, partnership is about *business*.

The Partnership Act 1890 – extracts and comments

The Partnership Act 1890 (which appears in the Appendix with other relevant legislation) encodes the law as it stood over 100 years ago. There is a public perception, shared by many advisers, that legislation which has stood for so long, must be sound and that firms may safely rely on its provisions. The Act is, however, a product of Victorian times and is in many respects inadequate for the demands of business at the end of the twentieth century. Indeed, the law (to an extent) recognises this by precluding partnerships of more than 20 individuals except for certain professional groups (see s 716 of the Companies Act 1985 in the Appendix).

The Act covers three main areas: relations with third parties; relations between partners; and dissolution. It is the second of these three areas which is of primary concern to the draftsman.

Relations between partners and implied terms

Sections 19 to 31 of the Act contain provisions which govern relations between partners. Those provisions constitute a set of 'default' rules which will be imposed on a partnership unless varied by the partners. Section 19 which deals with variations to the Agreement itself has already been referred to (see 'About the Precedents' above).

These provisions are worth examining in some detail, and may contain some surprises for the reader. Bear in mind that a *salaried partner* is often a partner for the purposes of the Act.

Interests and duties of partners

Section 24: **Rules as to interests and duties of partners subject to special agreement**

'The interests of partners in the partnership property and their rights and duties in relation to the partnership shall be determined, subject to any agreement express or implied between the partners, by the following rules:'

Thus, all of the provisions of this section can be varied or negated by agreement.

Section 24(1):

'All the partners are entitled to share equally in the capital and profits of the business, and must contribute equally towards the losses whether of capital or otherwise sustained by the firm.'

Note that according to the Act, both profits (or losses) *and capital* are shared equally. In many firms, the partners do not share profits and losses equally and, in some, a partner's shares of capital and of profits may be different.

In some firms, a partner may share in profits and losses but may not have to contribute to, or be entitled to share in, capital. This is generally not a desirable course of action, because it can give rise to disputes between partners over whether expenditure is of a capital nature or not, and problems concerning depreciation of capital assets. There is also a view that those who do not contribute to capital will not have sufficient commitment to the firm. Such partners are sometimes called 'Schedule D' partners because the main advantage of partnership to them may be in their being assessed to tax as self-employed, and paying reduced National Insurance contributions.

It is essential that the Agreement reflects precisely the parties' intention if the provisions of the Act are varied. Otherwise, you may have to handle, as I have done, the claim of a dismissed salaried partner for an equal share of the value of the firm's freehold building because of a badly drafted Agreement!

Section 24(5):
'Every partner may take part in the management of the partnership business.'

In larger firms – say more than 8 partners – some formal delegation of management is appropriate if the firm is to be run effectively.

Section 24(6):
'No partner shall be entitled to remuneration for acting in the partnership business.'

Whilst partnership salaries are comparatively unusual in professional firms, this subsection serves as a reminder that partners are not entitled as of right to drawings. As set out in s 1(1) of the Act (see 'Introduction' above) partnership is about making profit and, in the absence of agreement, partners cannot take drawings until a profit has been made – that is after accounts have been approved. There is also no obligation to work for the business which is why each Agreement needs a 'work full time' clause.

Section 24(7):
'No person may be introduced as a partner without the consent of all existing partners.'

A procedure for this needs to be set out in the Agreement.

Section 24(8):
'Any difference arising as to ordinary matters connected with the partnership business may be decided by a majority of the partners, but no change may be made in the nature of the partnership business without the consent of all existing partners.'

Careful consideration needs to be given to what constitutes 'ordinary' business. I refer you to Table M in Precedent 1: Standard Partnership Agreement and to the comments on management and decision making in 'About Drafting Agreements' (below).

Involuntary dissolution of the firm

Section 25: **Expulsion of partner**
'No majority of the partners can expel any partner unless a power to do so has been conferred by express agreement between the partners.'

There is no implied right to expel a partner from a partnership however good the cause: eg theft from the firm, imprisonment, absence or incapacity, removal of professional qualifications. The other partners' only remedy is to dissolve – even the court does not have power to expel a partner, only to dissolve the partnership. Indeed, such an event may cause dissolution of the firm whether the partners wish it or not.

Section 26: **Retirement from partnership at will**

'(1) Where no fixed term has been agreed upon for the duration of the partnership, any partner may determine the partnership at any time on giving notice of his intention so to do to all the other partners.

(2) Where the partnership has originally been constituted by deed, a notice in writing, signed by the partner giving it, shall be sufficient for this purpose.'

Section 32: **Dissolution by expiration or notice**

'Subject to any agreement between the partners, a partnership is dissolved –

(c) If entered into for an undefined time, by any partner giving notice to the other or others of his intention to dissolve the partnership.

In the last-mentioned case the partnership is dissolved as from the date mentioned in the notice as the date of dissolution, or, if no date is so mentioned, as from the date of the communication of the notice.'

Section 33: **Dissolution by bankruptcy, death or charge**

'(a) Subject to any agreement between the partners, every partnership is dissolved as regards all the partners by the death or bankruptcy of any partner.'

I have grouped these sections together because each can give rise to an involuntary dissolution of the firm.

Notice of termination may not need to be in writing (unless the Agreement is by deed). Therefore, a partner could turn up at a partners' meeting and announce that the partnership is at an end – now! No matter how unreasonable that partner might be, he or she would be quite within his or her rights.

On dissolution, the bank account is frozen immediately, the staff are redundant, the retainer of each client is automatically terminated and no partner or group of partners has any automatic right to take over the business and continue to run it. If the (now) former partners cannot agree how to deal with the dissolution, a receiver will be appointed by the court to dispose of the assets and distribute the proceeds among the former partners. Furthermore, if the 'closing year' provisions of the tax legislation are applied (if the firm is not yet on a current year basis of taxation – see 'Taxation' below), the Inland Revenue may impose additional taxation.

Likewise, the death or bankruptcy of one partner automatically dissolves the partnership unless there are contrary provisions in the Agreement. In such an event, the living, solvent partners will have to negotiate with either the executors or trustee in bankruptcy of the departed partner to try to keep the firm alive.

Accountability and duty not to compete

Section 29: **Accountability of partners for private profits**

'(1) Every partner must account to the firm for any benefit derived by him without the consent of the other partners from any transaction concerning the partnership, or from any use by him of the partnership property name or business connection.'

Section 30: **Duty of partner not to compete with firm**

'If a partner without the consent of the other partners, carries on any business of the same nature as and competing with that of the firm, he must account for and pay over to the firm all profits made by him in that business.'

There have been many cases where firms have taken action against individual partners who claim that the partnership premises do not belong to the firm.

Liability to third parties

Most partners will be aware that each partner in the firm is jointly liable with all the other partners for all the debts and liabilities of the partnership (s 9). Every partner is an agent of the firm for the purpose of its business and all actions of every partner in the normal course of the business bind all the other partners (s 5). It is less well understood that, even if it is agreed between the partners that one partner's authority is limited, that partner can nevertheless bind the firm unless the third party actually knows about the restriction (s 5). Notice received by any one partner is legally considered to be notice to the firm itself (s 16). Similarly, an admission or representation made by any one partner about the partnership may be used as evidence against the firm as a whole (s 15).

These and aspects of the liability of firms to and relationship with third parties are set out in ss 5 to 18 of the Act. Clearly, the effect of these sections cannot be varied by agreement between the partners, although the effect of most sections can be varied by agreement between the firm and the relevant third party. Sections 5 to 12 (in the Appendix) in particular, which set out the many ways in which a firm and therefore the partners may become personally liable for assorted obligations, should be read with special attention.

'Holding out'

Liability can also arise in two ways under s 14 which deals with 'holding out'.

Section 14:   **Persons liable by 'holding out'**

'(1) Every one who by words spoken or by conduct represents himself, or who knowingly suffers himself to be represented, as a partner in a particular firm, is liable as a partner to any one who has on the faith of any such representation given credit to the firm, whether the representation has or has not been made or communicated to the person so giving credit by or with the knowledge of the apparent partner making the representation or suffering it to be made.'

First, the person held out to be a partner is liable to third parties as a partner. Unless that person has acted outside the scope of his or her authority, he or she will be entitled to indemnity from the real partners – for what the indemnity is worth.

The second issue is that all of the partners who accede to the holding out are liable for whatever the 'held out' partner has committed the firm to and the 'held out' person is liable to third parties for whatever the real partners have committed to. Thus, the most junior salaried partner (who in truth may be no more than a salaried employee) is jointly liable with everyone else for the firm's debts even though he or she may never have attended a partners' meeting and may be in no position to influence any aspect of the firm's business. There is nothing any individual partner can do to protect himself or herself except by actually telling the third party that he or she is not liable. An exception often arises in the case of the firm's bankers (where exclusion of liability is common) and occasionally in the case of the firm's landlord.

I recommend also a specific exclusion with HM Customs & Excise in respect of VAT.

The moral is that those being offered partnership, particularly of a junior nature, should not accept without being sure that they can trust their senior partners and, preferably, having some idea of the firm's outstanding liabilities before they sign up. This latter point may be wishful thinking for those offered junior partnerships in major professional firms whose accounts are more carefully guarded than the Bank of England. A formal indemnity is, however, essential. Conversely, firms tempted to offer salaried partnerships with a view to staff retention should realise the extent to which the new 'partner' can commit them.

This doctrine of holding-out can also have unforeseen consequences for anyone who allows his or her name to be put on a partnership's notepaper unless it is quite clear from descriptive wording that he or she is not a partner. Thus, the old practice of drawing a line on the notepaper between equity and salaried partners does not exclude salaried partners from liability and the use of another title, eg 'Partnership secretary', might not exclude someone from liability if a third party believes that the title was descriptive of his or her role as a partner rather than indicating that he or she was not a partner.

Finally, risk continues for a retired partner who will continue to be held out as a partner until third parties who have dealt with the firm are made aware of his or her retirement. Sections 36 and 37 of the Partnership Act 1890 enable a retiring partner to cease to be held out by advertising in the *London Gazette*. However, such notice will not be sufficient to remove future liability for VAT. Section 45(2) of the Value Added Tax Act 1994 treats a retiring partner as continuing to be a partner for VAT purposes until the partnership change is notified to the Commissioners of Customs & Excise.

Assignment of profit shares

Section 31:   **Rights of assignee of share in partnership**

'(1) An assignment by any partner of his share in the partnership, either absolute or by way of mortgage or redeemable charge, does not, as against the other partners, entitle the assignee, during the continuance of the partnership, to interfere in the management or administration of the partnership business or affairs, or to require any accounts of the partnership transactions or to inspect the partnership books, but entitles the assignee only to receive the share of profits to which the assigning partner would otherwise be entitled, and the assignee must accept the account of profits agreed to by the partners.'

Partnership shares may, in the absence of a bar in a Partnership Agreement, be both assigned and charged. Assigning a share means selling or transferring the right to receive the partnership income to a third party. By charging is meant mortgaging the share to raise finance. Such mortgages normally contain a temporary assignment by way of security. An assignment gives only a legal right to receive income. In practice, it would undoubtedly confer influence. The rights assigned are much less than would be common in a modern mortgage.

In practice, very few firms would be prepared to suffer a third party having an ability to influence partnership matters, particularly in respect of the redistribution of shares. Moreover, for solicitors and some other professions, such an arrangement could constitute unprofessional conduct because it would enable a non-qualified person to share in the profits of the partnership. There can, of course, also be taxation complications if the assignee happens to be a corporate entity. Agreements for professional firms should therefore preclude assignment or charging.

Guarantees

Section 18:   **Revocation of continuing guaranty by change in firm**
'A continuing guaranty or cautionary obligation given either to a firm or to a third person in respect of the transactions of a firm is, in the absence of agreement to the contrary, revoked as to future transactions by any change in the constitution of the firm to which, or of the firm in respect of the transactions of which, the guaranty or obligation was given.'

Guarantees given to a firm or in respect of a firm are automatically revoked on a change in the constitution of the firm. Guarantees are distinguishable from the partners' joint and several liability. In practice, guarantees given by partnerships are relatively unusual and the section is not, therefore, as significant as it would at first appear. The section may be relevant where a third party has, for example, guaranteed payment of fees to a firm.

Liability of incoming and departing partners

Section 19:   **Variation by consent of terms of partnership**
'(1) A person who is admitted as a partner into an existing firm does not thereby become liable to the creditors of the firm for anything done before he became a partner.
(2) A partner who retires from the firm does not thereby cease to be liable for partnership debts or obligations incurred before his retirement.'

These two seemingly simple statements of principle often become blurred in practice. This is because almost every Retirement Deed and every Admission Deed of a new partner contain an obligation by the continuing partners (including the new partner) in favour of the previous partners to assume all the liabilities of the firm. Indeed, on retirement, an indemnity by the continuing partners is implied by law.

The significance of the obligation can most sharply be brought into focus in relation to professional negligence. If a firm is negligent, it is the *partners at the date of the negligent act* who are liable to the injured party – not those who are *partners at the time that the claim is made*. Retiring partners must ensure in these circumstances that they have indemnity from the continuing partners against claims which are made later and preferably that they have run-off insurance cover as well. Failing this, the retired partner (or his or her executors if he or she has died) may find themselves liable for a proportion of negligence claims without any recourse.

This issue has surfaced in another way recently. A client was a partner in a firm which took a lease of business premises in the early 1970s. Four partners signed the lease on behalf of the firm. Over the next 10 years, partners in the firm came and went (the client in question left two years later) and the firm effectively dissolved in about 1982. The four partners who signed the original lease have recently been sued, under their continuing liability as original tenants, as the current occupier has defaulted on rent payments. It is many years since the partnership ceased and the firm was, in any case, run most informally. Most of the partnership papers, if they ever existed, have been thrown away. Major problems are being caused in trying to decide which individuals, whether signatories to the lease or not (and in what proportions) are liable to contribute to the total liability of several hundred thousand pounds. It is essential that all agreements relating to continuing liabilities are recorded and retained indefinitely.

Dissolution

Sections 32 to 44 of the Partnership Act 1890 deal with dissolution. Sections 32 to 35 deal with the circumstances in which a firm can be wound up and ss 32 and 33 have already been discussed (see Involuntary dissolution of the firm above).

Section 38 gives useful clarification of the continuing authority of partners to wind up the firm after dissolution. Sections 39 to 44 deal with the financial rights between partners on dissolution or retirement. As these provisions do not affect third parties, they are capable of variation in the Partnership Agreement. The only section which requires specific reference is s 44.

Section 44: **Rule for distribution of assets on final settlement of accounts**
'In settling accounts between the partners after a dissolution of partnership, the following rules shall, subject to any agreement, be observed:
  (a) Losses, including losses and deficiencies of capital, shall be paid first out of profits, next out of capital, and lastly, if necessary, by the partners individually in the proportion in which they were entitled to share profits:
  (b) The assets of the firm including the sums, if any, contributed by the partners to make up losses or deficiencies of capital, shall be applied in the following manner and order:
    . . .
    4. The ultimate residue, if any, shall be divided among the partners in the proportion in which profits are divisible.'

Section 44 provides that such deficiencies and surpluses are provided and paid in profit ratios.

Clearly, this provision will need careful consideration for firms which have differing capital and profit ratios – and also for its implications on salaried partners. If capital and income shares are equal, it may be better to provide for distribution in capital ratios (to allow for temporary adjustments to profit shares, eg for maternity leave).

Other statutes

In the Appendix there are set out as well as the Partnership Act 1890 the following statutory extracts:
Business Names Act 1985 – which contains various rules on publicity relating to partnerships.
Companies Act 1985, s 716 – which limits partnerships to 20 partners apart from certain professions listed in the section and in statutory instruments (which are also listed).

Race Relations Act 1976, s 10.

Sex Discrimination Act 1975, s 11.

Income and Corporation Taxes Act 1988, s 111 (Finance Act 1994, s 215) – which sets out the revised basis of assessment for income tax for partners coming into effect between 1994 and 1998.

Value Added Tax Act 1994, s 45.

Taxation

It is beyond the scope of this work to consider taxation law relating to partnerships, except insofar as it affects the Agreement between partners.

The Finance Act 1994, s 215 (replacing the Income and Corporation Taxes Act 1988, s 111) has effected a major change in the law. Prior to the passing of s 215, the majority of partnerships were assessed to income tax on a preceding year basis of assessment (that is to say that the tax assessment for the current year is based on profits earned in an earlier year). The significant aspects of the old law (apart from its complexity when there have been changes in partners or in profit shares from one year to the next) are twofold.

The first is that it is a *partnership* assessment. In other words the assessment is a joint and several liability of the partners in the year of assessment (not in the year that the profits were earned). Because of the complexity of the law, and delays in finalising partnership accounts, assessments can take years to be finalised. As a result, Partnership Agreements contain standard clauses enabling the firm to make reserves and retentions from current and retired partners to meet the firm's tax liability.

The second is that the legislation also has special provisions for the *opening and closing years* of a firm's activities. These can have the effect of moving the assessment from an actual or current year basis to a preceding year basis after a firm has started in business and back to a current year basis as it ceases. Under the legislation, a firm ceases each time a new partner is admitted or an existing partner retires, unless a continuation election is signed by all partners. For this reason, Agreements contain provisions enabling the continuing partners to decide whether a continuation election should be used, subject to suitable indemnities.

Section 215 has removed both of these problems. The provisions come into force immediately for all firms commencing after 6 April 1994; upon a cessation after that date if there is no election to continue; and in any case in the tax year 1997–98 – that is after 5 April 1997 (there are transitional provisions). After the provisions come into force for a firm there will be no more partnership assessments (apart from past years). Each partner will be assessed individually on his or her share of the profits, with no joint and several liability for the firm. Assessments to tax will be on a current year basis and so the concept of an election to continue will disappear.

Even though the firm will have no continuing liability for an individual partner's tax, I still strongly recommend that funds should be retained from partners' capital accounts or drawings to meet their individual tax bills. Some partners may not be able to resist the temptation to spend their tax reserve, with consequent financial pressures being put on the firm. In any case, with a current year basis the tax is likely to be assessed and partly paid (albeit on an estimated basis) before the accounts for a given year are signed! The precedents are drawn on the basis of such a tax retention.

As to Value Added Tax, it is important to register in the names of equity partners to avoid salaried partners being liable, and to remember that specific notice of a partner leaving *must* be given for him or her to avoid future liability (see s 45(2) of the Value Added Tax Act 1994 under 'holding out' above).

ABOUT DRAFTING AGREEMENTS

It is a truism to say that most partners in most firms never look at their Partnership Agreement once it has been drawn up. Some, I suspect, do not even read it before signing it. For some partners, reading the document may cause heart failure! For others, it is barely necessary to look at the document because it records principles which the partners have already discussed and understood.

Time spent considering what should go into a Partnership Agreement is absolutely crucial to the success of any firm. It is essential for the partners, or prospective partners, to agree how they will go about taking decisions and what will happen if one of them leaves. Agreement on these issues at the beginning of the business relationship is a good guarantee of its continuing success. Failure to consider these matters or, even worse, failure to agree upon them is a formula for future disharmony.

Whilst the flexibility of partnership is one of its main virtues, it is also the source of major problems. Most firms start small and the partners are tempted not to have any written Agreement drawn when they start. There is no such thing as an off-the-shelf Partnership Agreement; even the most straightforward Agreement being more expensive to prepare than buying a ready-made company (although naturally I hope that this book will go some way towards reducing the cost). In the early days, partners in a new venture inevitably get on well with each other and assume that problems can be dealt with as and when they arise.

Sometimes, problems are so serious that if they had been addressed in the first place it is possible that the partners would never have gone into business together. For example, some years ago I was retained by a four-partner firm to prepare their Partnership Agreement. Two of the partners had been running the business for many years and the other two had been brought in some four or five years previously and were some 20 years younger. It became apparent in the course of discussions that the expectations of the older partners as to their entitlement to goodwill payments and annuities on retirement were so different to the perceptions of the younger partners that the firm broke up.

Of course, Agreements have their limitations. There is very little which can be inserted in a Partnership Agreement to limit liability, apart from setting out the limits of individual partner's authority and providing indemnities for breach. To be effective, arrangements to limit liability must be negotiated direct with the relevant third party – the bank, the landlord, Customs & Excise, and so on (see 'Liability to third parties' in 'About the Law' above).

A number of drafting tips appear both in 'About the Law' (above) and in notes to the various precedents. I hope also that the Checklist (below) will assist the process of discussion and clarification.

The topic of 'Management and Decision-making' needs the most careful consideration. It is desirable to define which issues are to have a majority vote, and which require unanimity. Agreements have to set out detailed voting procedures, those for medium to large firms clarifying whether votes are to be cast according to partnership shares rather than one person one vote, and whether or not different majorities are required for different types of resolutions. Votes requiring a 75% majority (akin to a company's Special Resolution) are common and indeed some American professional firms tend now to refer to their 'shareholders' rather than their partners. In almost all firms (except the smallest), efficient management requires some authority to be delegated to individuals and committees.

Striking the right balance between the majority oppressing the minority and 'the tail wagging the dog' is an art rather than a science. A firm must be protected against one partner preventing progress by vetoing, for example, a move to new premises or in a larger firm the introduction of a new partner. However, a partner should not be victimised by, for example, a majority deciding to reduce his profit share. On the merger of two small firms the partners drew up their own Partnership Agreement. The Agreement stated that the previous senior partner of one of the firms should, from the date of merger, become a salaried partner in the new firm and he was required to sign the new Partnership Agreement – which did not deal with voting issues. Describing a partner as a salaried partner only determines what share of the income of the firm he or she is entitled to; it does not affect capital or voting. In this case, substantial problems were created because the former senior partner found himself holding the voting balance in the new firm – very much 'the tail wagging the dog'!

In all firms, except the very smallest, a power to remove a partner without cause (subject to suitable safeguards) is essential to deal with the situation where a firm is threatened because one partner is no longer in tune with the rest. In the absence of agreement, there is no way of terminating the partnership of a partner who is incompetent or idle or who is a former 'high flier' crashed to earth. The other partners are exposed to the risk of negligence actions and loss of goodwill with their clients, or profits may be unfairly distributed. Businesses operating under the Companies Acts have a distinct advantage here – no one is immune from dismissal after passing an ordinary resolution of which special notice has been given.

In the absence of agreement, there is no right for any partner to take drawings on account of profit share until the accounts are signed – at which point the year's share must be paid out. Clearly, Agreements must make provisions for drawings; and for suitable reserves for contingencies, particularly taxation.

And finally, the Agreement must deal in detail with the circumstances in which the firm may be dissolved, and what is to happen to its assets (including trading name, goodwill, premises and clients) on dissolution.

To conclude, as I have said in the opening section of this introduction 'Partnership is about relationships between individuals'. Partnerships will succeed if they are based on informed agreement and mutual confidence and trust between the partners. Without this they will fail, no matter how well the Agreement is drafted.

PARTNERSHIP AGREEMENT CHECKLIST[1]

There follows a checklist of considerations which the practitioner should discuss with the prospective partners when contemplating the preparation of the Partnership Agreement. The checklist is divided into the following sections:

---

[1] Many of these questions may not be relevant to a two-person partnership.

1. ABOUT THE BUSINESS	
Trading name	
Trading address	
When commenced (or new)?	
Number of partners	
Is it likely ever to have only two partners?[2]	
Trade or profession	
Special features of the business (eg regulatory rules; treatment of stock or work in progress; commission income)[3]	
Provide copies of: 1 last Accounts 2 any existing agreements	
Name and Address of Partnership Accountants	
Why is a partnership required rather than a limited company?	

[2] Special clauses need to be inserted into two-partner Partnership Agreements, in particular to deal with events following dissolution (see Precedent 3: Two-partner Firm Partnership Agreement, Schedule T at p 105).

[3] See 3. Financial Arrangements below.

2. ABOUT THE PARTNERS AND THEIR BENEFITS	
All Partners[4]	
Holiday entitlement	
Incapacity: 1 leave period at full profit share 2 any reduced share period? 3 leave period before termination	
Maternity leave: 1 periods of full profit share 2 periods of partial profit share	
Amount of compulsory contribution to pensions	
Compulsory medicals?	
Rights to receive related financial benefits[5]	
Are there any 'sleeping' partners?[6]	

---

[4]   In some firms, there may be different arrangements for different partners. In such cases, these should be noted on individual partner's information from under 'Special Rights'.

[5]   Include eg lecture fees, publications, legacies, family company fees.

[6]   See Precedent 4: Trading Firm Partnership Agreement, Schedule I (definition of 'Investing Partners') at p 128, and Clause M4.3 at p 132.

Each Partner	
Full name	
Private address	
Identifying initials	
Age/date of birth	
Profit share (%) Prior or special share (eg salary)[7]	
Capital share (%) Amount £	
Drawings limit	
Any pension or annuity from firm on retirement – how calculated?	
Goodwill entitlement	
Special role (eg Senior Partner)	
Special rights[8]	

---

[7] See Precedent 4: Trading Firm Partnership Agreement, Clause F2.1 at p 122.

[8] Here note eg part-time working obligations, outside business interests, special voting rights, sickness leave, holiday entitlement etc.

3. FINANCIAL ARRANGEMENTS	
Total capital	
Capital 'equalisation provisions'	
Basis of provision of further capital	
Arrangements for profit share variation	
Accounting year end	
Taxation: 1 is firm still on preceding year basis? 2 will partners continue to reserve for tax when on actual basis?[9]	
Special accounting requirements[10]	
Advances by partners to the firm: 1 interest rate 2 notice period to withdraw and amount	
Bank mandate	
Division of profits on dissolution – in profit shares or capital shares?	

---

[9] I recommend that firms continue to reserve for and pay partner's tax, even after the firm's liability ceases under the Income and Corporation Taxes Act 1988, s 111 (see Appendix). See eg Precedent 1: Standard Partnership Agreement, Clause F8.1 at p 38.

[10] Insert accounting requirements unique to the business or the firm. For example, basis of valuation of goodwill (if in account), stock or work in progress valuation, depreciation (if a partner's capital share differs from his or her profit share) and provisions for capital revaluations. Some of these items may only be relevant to payments by new partners or to departed partners.

4. MANAGEMENT AND ADMINISTRATION	
Partners' meetings notice period	
Quorum 1 number or percentage 2 must quorum be present for whole meeting	
Proxy votes?[11]	
Voting eligibility[12]	
Is there to be a Senior Partner and what authority does he or she have?	
Is there to be a Managing Partner and what authority does he or she have?[13]	
Any other management delegation?	
Resolutions: 1 what votes on what resolutions?[14] 2 are any percentages other than 51, 75 and 100 required?	

[11] Partners tend to have strongly divided views as to the desirability of proxy voting. Such a provision is desirable in larger firms, and important if a very high percentage is adopted for quorum to avoid inquorate meetings.

[12] It is important to specify whether percentages are by those attending a meeting or by total number of partners whether or not attending.

[13] See Precedent 4: Trading Firm Partnership Agreement, Clause M4 at p 131.

[14] Check percentages per Table M in Precedent 1: Standard Partnership Agreement, at p 47.

5. PARTNERS LEAVING	
Restrictive covenants: 1 staff – for how long? 2 clients – for how long? 3 non compete – time? distance?	
Retirement age	
By notice – differentiate retirement and resignation?[15]	
Period before retirement due to incapacity (see '2. About the Partners and their Benefits – All Partners' above)	
Compulsory retirement provisions required?[16]	
Suspension provisions required?[17]	
Will sole remaining partner have option to continue business?[18]	

[15] This will be relevant if there is a financial penalty for leaving before say age 55, eg having to wait for capital.

[16] Compulsory retirement is intended to be used to remove a partner on a 'no fault' basis. See Precedent 1: Standard Partnership Agreement, Clause T8 at p 60.

[17] This may be inappropriate for firms of less than five partners.

[18] See Precedent 2: Small Firm Partnership Agreement, Clause T4 at p 88.

6. FINANCIAL ARRANGEMENTS ON PARTNERS LEAVING	
At what rate are repayments of the following made?	
Advances	
Profit share to date of leaving	
Retirement capital	
Retirement interest	
How are these times varied for?	
Retirement	
Resignation	
Incapacity	
Expulsion[19]	
Death	
Any goodwill payment on leaving?[20] If so, how calculated?	

[19] Is there any other 'penalty' on expulsion, eg no interest?
[20] Generally not recommended but see Precedent 4: Trading Firm Partnership Agreement, Clause T5 at p 139.

PRECEDENT 1: STANDARD PARTNERSHIP AGREEMENT FOR A PROFESSIONAL FIRM

CONTENTS

PRECEDENT 1: STANDARD PARTNERSHIP AGREEMENT FOR A PROFESSIONAL FIRM[1]

THIS PARTNERSHIP AGREEMENT[2] executed as a Deed[3] constitutes the terms on which the Partners have agreed to carry on business in partnership as [*trade or profession*] and is intended to be known as

THE [*name of firm*] 199[. . .] PARTNERSHIP AGREEMENT[4]

1.   THE SCHEDULES
      This Agreement includes the following Schedules and Tables:

Schedule D[5]	which contains **D**issolution provisions
Schedule F	which contains **F**inancial provisions
Table F	which contains details of capital profit shares and drawings
Schedule I	which contains **I**nterpretation of this Agreement and definitions used in this Agreement
Schedule M	which contains **M**eetings' procedure and voting arrangements
Table M	which contains details of voting percentages
Schedule P	which contains **P**artners' names and addresses
Schedule R	which contains **R**epayment arrangements on termination
Schedule T	which contains **T**ermination and Suspension provisions
Schedule V	which contains **V**ariations and waivers affecting individual Partners

---

[1] This precedent is a full form suitable for up to approximately 20 partners. It does not contain clauses appropriate to a firm which might have only two partners, as to which see Precedent 2: Small Firm Partnership Agreement, at p 65.

[2] See 'About the Precedents' in the Introduction which describes the numbering system used in the precedents. First-time users of this precedent should read Schedule I (Interpretation) first.

[3] The Agreement is executed as a deed (Schedule X) to give effect to the following clauses:
   4.3   indemnity as to private debts;
   5.2   trust of property (desirable not essential);
   5.3   property indemnity;
   5.4   removal of property trustee and grant of power of attorney;
   11.1   appointment of partner as attorney to sign on behalf of firm;
   F8.2 and F8.5   tax election;
   F8.3 and F8.4   tax indemnities.

[4] As the Agreement may initially be executed by partners on different days, and subsequently amended and executed by new partners, it is identified by a name, and not dated. See 'About the Precedents' in the Introduction and the Partnership Act 1890, s 19 (see Appendix) as to variation of partnership deeds.

[5] See note 2 above.

Schedule X   which contains e**X**ecution of this Agreement by the Partners

2.   DURATION – FIRM NAME

2.1   The Partnership shall continue until terminated in accordance with the provisions of this Agreement

2.2   The Partnership shall be carried on under the Firm Name or such other name or names as the Partners shall Resolve[6]

3.   CHANGES OF PARTNERS

3.1   No person shall be admitted as a Partner otherwise than by a Resolution of the Partners in favour of the introduction of the new Partner and the terms of the introduction

3.2   No merger of the Partnership with another firm shall take place otherwise than by a Resolution of the Partners

3.3   No person shall be appointed as a salaried partner otherwise than by a Resolution of the Partners[7]

3.4   Any person becoming a Partner shall signify his or her acceptance of this Agreement by signing as a Deed in Schedule X opposite the entry of his or her name and his or her name address identifying initials and date of joining shall be inserted in Schedule P

3.5   If any Partner shall cease to be a Partner then the Partnership shall not be dissolved as to the other Partners unless as a result thereof only one Partner remains

3.6   There shall be inserted in Schedule P against the entry of the name of any person who has ceased to be a Partner the date upon which he or she so ceased

4.   GENERAL DUTIES OF THE PARTNERS

4.1   Each Partner shall be just and faithful to the other Partners in all transactions dealings and matters relating to or affecting the Partnership and shall in all circumstances give a true and proper account thereof when reasonably required so to do by any of the other Partners

4.2   Each Partner shall devote the whole of his or her time and attention to the business of the Firm [subject to Clause F2 and Schedule V][8] and diligently and faithfully employ himself or herself therein and use his or her best

---

[6] 'Resolve' and 'Resolution' are defined terms. See definitions in Schedule I at p 43 and Table M at p 47.

[7] This clause is not essential as 'Salaried Partners' are normally not true partners in the firm. They are not bound by the terms of this Agreement as they are not parties to it. A form of salaried partners agreement is strongly recommended (see Precedent 7: Salaried Partners Agreement, at p 153). However, many firms do not have such an agreement possibly in part from a desire not to emphasise to salaried partners how little benefit they get and how much risk they have undertaken.

[8] If there are a number of part-time partners, it may be appropriate to amend this clause, Clause F2 and Table F and/or Schedule V to list their time commitment. For an alternative approach, see Precedent 4: Trading Firm Partnership Agreement, Clause 4.2 at p 116 and Schedule P at p 135.

endeavours to carry on the same for the utmost benefit of the Partnership[9]

4.3 Each Partner shall at all times duly and punctually pay and discharge his or her separate and private debts and engagements whether present or future and keep the property of the Partnership and the other Partners and their personal representatives estates and effects indemnified therefrom and from all actions proceedings costs claims and demands in respect thereof

5. PARTNERSHIP PROPERTY

5.1 The Partnership shall be carried on at [*address* and at][10] such places as the Partners shall Resolve

5.2 Any premises from time to time used for the purpose of the Partnership and property or securities or other assets of whatsoever kind held by the Partnership at the date hereof or hereafter acquired on behalf of the Partnership shall be the property of the Partnership and shall be held by such of the Partners in whose names the same may from time to time be vested in trust for the Partners in the shares in which they are from time to time entitled to share in capital

5.3 The Partners hereby indemnify any Partner or former Partner in whose name any such property or securities or other assets as aforesaid are for the time being vested (or have previously been vested) against all claims for rent property taxes costs of repairs alterations or improvements and insurance relating to any such property and generally in respect of any obligations in respect of any such property securities or other assets[11]

5.4 Without prejudice to any statutory power if any Partner shall cease to be a Partner the other Partners may by deed[12] remove him or her from the trusteeship and by the same or any other deed or deeds may appoint one or more other persons (whether or not being the person or persons exercising the power) to be a trustee or trustees in place of the Partner so removed from the trusteeship and may by the same or another deed grant power of attorney to the person or persons so appointed in the name of the Partner so removed to execute any document necessary to vest the property comprised in the trust in the new trustees thereof[13]

---

[9] There is no requirement under the Partnership Act 1890 for any partner to devote any specific amount of time to the firm's business.

[10] Traditional partnership agreements include the address of the firm premises but this may not be necessary unless there are special circumstances.

[11] Although such an indemnity is implied, an express indemnity is better. As a result of the recession in the early 1990s, a number of ex-partners have found themselves being sued on leases they signed for their firms many years ago, often without any formal documentation still in existence to prove their indemnity rights. Put a copy of your Partnership Agreement with your will!

[12] Note that under Clause 11.1 the senior partner has power of attorney to execute the deeds.

[13] Changes of title to property on partnership changes are often overlooked, and obtaining signatures later can be difficult, expensive and sometimes impossible particularly if a partner has not left on good terms. This clause and the two preceding clauses are all good reasons to execute the Agreement under seal.

6.   HOLIDAYS – INCAPACITY – PREGNANCY AND MEDICAL
        EXAMINATION

6.1   Each Partner shall be entitled (in addition to statutory holidays) to [four] weeks holiday in each calendar year or to such other periods as the Partners may from time to time Resolve

6.2   Without prejudice to the provisions of Clauses F2 and T6 any Partner who shall be incapacitated (except by reason of pregnancy) from carrying out his or her duties for a total of [125 working days][14] in any period of [18 months] shall be automatically suspended from acting as a Partner until he or she shall be certified by a doctor as fit to resume full-time work and shall have resumed his or her duties

6.3   A Partner who becomes pregnant shall:

        6.3.1   be entitled to up to [125 working days] leave of absence. Up to 55 working days of such leave may be taken prior to the expected date of confinement but the period of leave may commence earlier if a doctor certifies that it should. Such absence shall not affect her holiday entitlement

        6.3.2   give to her other Partners as much notice as is reasonable in the circumstances of her expected date of confinement the date on which she expects to leave work and the date on which she expects to return to work

        6.3.3   be entitled to a modified share of profits in accordance with Clause F2

        6.3.4   be automatically suspended from acting as a Partner if she shall not return to work at the end of her period of leave of absence until she shall be certified by a doctor as fit to resume full-time work and shall have resumed her duties[15]

6.4   Each Partner shall arrange for a medical examination by a competent medical adviser at least once in any period of 2 years and such Partner shall authorise such medical adviser to supply a copy of the report to [the Senior Partner][16]

6.5   [The Senior Partner] may in consultation with another Partner require a Partner to take such action as may be recommended in the report referred to in Clause 6.4 or to submit to a further examination by a medical adviser nominated by [the Senior Partner] and thereafter to take such action as may be recommended by the nominated medical adviser[17]

---

[14] Quote periods of absence in working days rather than months. This prevents a sick partner from appearing at the office on a stretcher for a day or two, in order to start the six months' sick leave again!

[15] Consideration might be given to paternity leave. 10 working days is considered an appropriate period.

[16] See Clause M5 at p 46.

[17] This clause and the preceding clause are designed to give firms early warning of impending medical problems for partners, especially those which are stress-related. These two clauses may be inappropriate for smaller firms (eg up to say six partners).

7. PARTNER'S INSURANCE

7.1 Unless otherwise Resolved by the Partners every Partner shall make provision for retirement through the medium of retirement annuities or personal pension schemes by applying in each Accounting Period not less than [17.5%] of his or her profit share before taxation for the previous Accounting Period (not exceeding the maximum amount allowed under Sections 619 and 640 of the Income and Corporation Taxes Act 1988 as amended from time to time) in payment of premiums therefor or contributions thereto[18]

7.2 Each Partner shall make payment for such permanent disability insurance life insurance and other personal insurances as the Partners shall from time to time Resolve[19]

8. RESTRICTIONS

Subject to the provisions of this Agreement and unless otherwise Resolved no Partner shall:

8.1 engage directly or indirectly in any business other than that of the Firm. A Partner shall be deemed to be engaged in any business (not being a company whose shares are quoted on a recognised stock exchange) if such Partner directly or indirectly has an investment in that business or has loaned moneys to that business or entered into guarantees on behalf of that business[20]

8.2 engage or (except for gross misconduct) dismiss any member of the staff of the Firm (other than staff working specifically for that Partner and then only after following due statutory and Partnership procedures)[21]

---

[18] Many professional firms now insist on partners making adequate provision for their retirement through personal pension plans. Many partners argue that this is not an area in which the other partners should interfere; that provision for retirement should be a matter for the choice of each partner. I disagree. Substantial moral pressure can be placed upon partners when a partner who has not made adequate provision reaches retirement age, to make some special arrangement as the partner cannot afford to retire. In firms where progression to larger equity shares is by negotiation, older partners are not willing to reduce their profit shares because they need the earnings to provide for pension. Similarly, problems can arise if partners die before retirement or retire due to ill health without having made adequate provision. For all of these reasons, provisions requiring partners to contribute to pension are essential. Pension provision is a very tax-effective form of investment for the self-employed. Premiums (up to the statutory limit) are fully deductible for income tax, and the resultant cash at retirement is tax free as to capital withdrawn and earned income as to pension.

[19] Similar considerations to those set out in the note to the preceding paragraph apply. However, I do not consider it essential to set out the detailed requirements, which will vary substantially from one firm to another, in the Agreement.

[20] It is assumed that partners will work full time for the firm. Individual waivers and variations can be listed in Schedule V. Many partnership problems arise because of involvement of individual partners in outside business enterprises, and these should be discouraged, unless they are for the direct benefit of the firm. If they are for the direct benefit of the firm, perhaps the earnings should be brought in as partnership profits under Clause F2.4.

[21] In any but the smallest firms, management authority is delegated to an individual partner or committee, and individual partners should be restrained from treating the firm as their private fief.

8.3   employ any of the money goods or effects of the Firm or pledge the credit thereof except in the ordinary course of business and upon the account or for the benefit of the Firm

8.4   lend money or give credit on behalf of the Firm to or have any dealings with any person firm or company whom the Partners shall have previously Resolved not to treat or deal with and any loss incurred through any breach of this provision shall be made good to the Firm by the Partner incurring the same

8.5   buy order or contract for any goods articles or property on behalf of the Firm in excess of [£1,000] in any one transaction and any goods articles or property bought ordered or contracted for by any Partner in breach of this provision shall be taken and paid for by that Partner and shall be his or her separate property unless the Partners shall Resolve to adopt the transaction on behalf of the Partnership[22]

8.6   enter into any bond or become bail surety or security with or for any person or do or knowingly cause or suffer to be done any thing whereby the Partnership property or any part thereof may be seized attached or taken in execution[23]

8.7   enter into any obligation which cannot be honoured out of assets other than the interest of the Partner in the Firm at the time when such obligation is entered into[24]

8.8   assign mortgage or charge his or her share in the Partnership or any part of such share[25]

[9.   **PREVIOUS AGREEMENTS**
Save in respect of continuing obligations to former Partners the previous Partnership Agreement dated [. . .] [(as varied by Resolution)] shall forthwith cease to have effect]

10.   **VARIATION OF AGREEMENT**
10.1   Subject as herein otherwise expressly provided the terms and provisions of this Agreement relating to financial matters (including by way of example but not of limitation shares of profit contributions to capital and repayment of capital) or voting rights may be varied by Resolution of the Partners

---

[22] See note 21 above.

[23] Another aspect of the unlimited liability of partners is that the firm is at risk of having its assets attacked if a partner does not meet his or her personal obligations. This clause would give grounds for expulsion if the firm's assets were attacked by a partner's creditors. Expulsion would not necessarily be justified if there was no real risk to the firm.

[24] See note 23 above.

[25] Assigning a share does not make the assignee a partner. It merely gives him or her a right to receive a share of the profits, not to act as partner. See the Partnership Act 1890, s 31 (see Appendix).

10.2   Subject as herein otherwise expressly provided any other terms and conditions of this Agreement may also be varied by Resolution of the Partners

10.3   No variation pursuant to this Clause shall take effect so as to prejudice the rights of any former Partner

10.4   In the event of any dispute as to percentage of votes required to pass any Resolution for any variation of the Agreement pursuant to this Clause the decision of [the Senior Partner] as to the relevant percentage shall be final

10.5   Upon any variation of this Agreement amendments shall be made to the relevant page or pages or a new page or new pages shall be inserted in the Agreement and in either case shall be signed by [the Senior Partner or the Managing Partner]. A copy of the page or pages as amended or substituted shall be supplied to each Partner as soon as practical after signature[26]

10.6   Variations of this Agreement affecting individual Partners resolved upon by the Partners are set out in Schedule V

11.   GENERAL

11.1   [The Senior Partner] for the time being is hereby appointed attorney in the name of and on behalf of the Partnership authorised to enter into any agreement and to sign and deliver any deed and do any act or thing on behalf of the Partners which is properly authorised pursuant to the terms of this Agreement and a certificate purporting to be under the hand of the [Senior Partner] for the time being shall be sufficient evidence in favour of any person having dealings with the Firm of the authority of the [Senior Partner] named in such certificate to act under this provision[27]

11.2   Save as herein otherwise provided all disputes and questions whatsoever which shall either during the Partnership or afterwards arise between the Partners or their respective personal representatives or between any Partners or Partner and the representatives of any other Partners touching these presents or the construction or application thereof or any account valuation or division of assets debts or liabilities to be made hereunder or as to any act deed or omission of any Partner or as to any other matter in any way relating to the Partnership or the affairs thereof or the rights duties

---

[26]   This clause gives effect to the loose-leaf principles of this form of Agreement. This Agreement will be executed with one master copy and copies held by partners in a ring binder which can be updated as appropriate. I recommend that each page of the original document should be initialled by one partner for identification purposes. It is recommended that original pages which are amended are retained with the master copy. See 'About the Precedents' in the Introduction and the Partnership Act 1890, s 19.

[27]   This clause is intended to give the senior partner (or other named partner) power of attorney to sign documents on behalf of the firm. This can simplify the execution of documents and help to deal with emergencies. However, despite the wording of the clause, some firms do not like this provision as it can create the impression that the senior partner has *carte blanche* to commit the firm. For this clause to be effective, the Agreement should be executed as a deed.

or liabilities of any person under this Agreement shall be referred to a single arbitrator who shall be appointed by the Partners involved in the dispute if they can agree upon one or (failing agreement) by the [President for the time being of the [*name of body*]] on the application of any Partner or personal representative and in either case in accordance with and subject to the provisions of the Arbitration Acts 1950 to 1979[28]

11.3   Any notice authorised or required to be given or served by this Agreement shall be deemed to be duly served if the same shall be delivered personally to the person to whom it is intended to be given or shall be sent by post in a pre-paid letter sent by recorded delivery or by registered post and addressed to him or her either at his or her last known place of abode in England or (if it is reasonable to expect that he or she will receive it within 72 hours) left for him or her in the room of the Partnership premises in which he or she habitually worked as a Partner and where so sent or left shall be deemed to be served on the first working day of the Firm which shall follow the day on which such letter would in the ordinary course of post have been delivered or the day on which the same shall have been left

11.4   A notice to the Partners shall be properly served if delivered to or served upon the [Senior Partner] (or in the case of notice by the [Senior Partner], upon the [Managing] Partner) in accordance with this Clause

---

[28]   Partnership disputes before the courts should be avoided. Arbitration is a most suitable procedure for partners. Some firms name the arbitrator in their Agreement, often their solicitor.

SCHEDULE D

Dissolution Provisions

D1   RESOLUTION TO DISSOLVE

The Partnership may be dissolved by a Resolution[29] of the Partners and shall be dissolved in accordance with Clause 3.5[30]

D2   DISTRIBUTION OF NET ASSETS

Upon the dissolution of the Partnership the assets and credits shall be sold or realised as soon as practicable and the proceeds applied

D2.1   first in paying and discharging the debts and liabilities of the Partnership and the expenses of and incidental to the winding up of the affairs of the Partnership any deficiency being contributed rateably by the Partners in the proportions in which they shared profits[31] immediately prior to dissolution

D2.2   second in paying to those Partners who have made Advances [and Tax Reserves] the amount of such Advances [and Tax Reserves] together with interest accrued on such Advances [and Tax Reserves] in accordance with Clause[s] F7.1 [and F8.1] up to the date of dissolution and as between such Partners rateably according to the total of such Advances [and Tax Reserves]

D2.3   third in repaying to the Partners rateably their Capital Accounts but so that no payment shall be made to a Partner whose Capital Account is less than his or her due proportion until repayments of Capital Account to other Partners have reduced their Capital Accounts to a similar proportional level

D2.4   last in paying any surplus rateably to the Partners in the proportions in which they shared profits[32] immediately prior to dissolution

D3   EXECUTION OF DOCUMENTS

The Partners respectively shall execute do or concur in all necessary or proper instruments acts matters and things for effecting or facilitating the

---

[29] 'Resolve' and 'Resolution' are defined terms. See definitions in Schedule I at p 43 and Table M at p 47.

[30] Clause 3.5 provides for dissolution if there is only one partner. If it is likely that the firm may reduce to only two or three partners, consider using Precedent 2: Small Firm Partnership Agreement or adapting Clause T4 (and related clauses) from it dealing with succession in these circumstances.

[31] Note that profit shares determine the contribution to any deficiency and the distribution of any surplus on dissolution. Consideration should be given to amending these clauses if capital shares differ from profit shares.

[32] See note 31 above.

getting in sale and realisation of the assets and credits of the Partnership and the due application and division of the proceeds thereof and for their mutual release or indemnity or otherwise

D4   RESTRICTION ON USE OF FIRM'S NAME
          No Partner shall be entitled to practise after the date of dissolution under the Firm Name unless and to the extent that he or she shall have been authorised to do so by all[33] of the other Partners

---

[33]   Some larger firms might prefer a smaller majority than 'all' for this provision to enable a substantial majority of the partners to re-form under the firm name in the event of a major dispute giving rise to dissolution. Perhaps it would be appropriate to use the same percentage as in Clause D1. I would not recommend any less percentage than 100% in firms of less than, say, 10 partners to avoid abuse of the minority (as to which see 'About Drafting Agreements' in the Introduction).

SCHEDULE F

Financial Provisions

F1   CAPITAL[34]
F1.1   The capital of the Partnership shall be the amount[35] contributed as set out in Table F or such other amount as the Partners shall Resolve[36]

F1.2   Any further capital required by the Partnership shall be contributed by the Partners in the proportions in which they are entitled to share in profits

F2   PROFIT SHARES[37]
F2.1   The profits of the Partnership after payment of interest pursuant to Clause F7.1 [and Clause F8.1] shall be divided between the Partners in the shares set out against the name of each Partner in Table F subject to the provisions of this Clause and Clause F4

F2.2   In respect of a Partner who is incapacitated from carrying out his or her duties (except by reason of pregnancy) for the period set out in Clause 6.2 the profit share due to such Partner shall cease to accrue to such Partner from the end of such period of incapacity until he or she shall have resumed his or her duties in accordance with Clause 6.2

F2.3   In respect of a Partner who is entitled to leave of absence by reason of pregnancy pursuant to Clause 6.3
          F2.3.1   for the first [3] months[38] of such absence the Partner shall be entitled to her full profit share
          F2.3.2   for the next [3] months of such absence the Partner shall [not be entitled to any profit share] and
          F2.3.3   during any further period of absence the Partner shall not be entitled to any further profit share unless such absence arises through incapacity (in which case the provisions of Clause 6.2 relating to incapacity will apply) or for holiday to which that Partner is entitled[39]

---

[34]   Partners are not entitled to interest on capital before signature of the Firm's Accounts (Partnership Act 1890, s 24(4)). Inequality of contribution can be dealt with either by treating part of the capital as an advance under Clause F7 or inserting a provision for payment of interest on capital.

[35]   See note 46 below as to reserves.

[36]   'Resolve' and 'Resolution' are defined terms. See definitions in Schedule I at p 43 and Table M at p 47.

[37]   See Precedent 4: Trading Firm Partnership Agreement, Clause F2 at p 122 for an example of Partners' 'salaries' plus profit share.

[38]   These periods are suggested as a minimum recommendation.

[39]   It may be appropriate to insert a further sub-clause here, if there are a number of part-time partners (see Clause 4.2 at p 26). Alternatively, it may be appropriate to insert a variation in Schedule V.

F2.4   All sums received by a Partner as the holder of any office or appointment
            where his or her holding of such office or appointment is occasioned by
            reason of him or her being a [*profession*] shall belong to the Firm (and any
            time spent or expenses incurred in the performance of his or her duties in
            respect of such office or appointment shall be deemed to have been spent
            or incurred on behalf of the Firm) but this provision shall not apply to any
            of the following:
            [F2.4.1   any gift of a specific chattel to a Partner
            F2.4.2   any legacy bequeathed to a Partner by will or codicil
            F2.4.3   any payment received by a Partner as a director or other officer or
                     member of any private family company or business belonging to
                     his or her family
            F2.4.4   any sum received by a Partner for authorship or lecturing
            F2.4.5   any sum received for television or radio broadcasting][40]

F3   DRAWINGS
            Each Partner shall be at liberty to draw out for his or her separate use on
            account of his or her accruing profit share for the then current Accounting
            Period the monthly amount set against his or her name in Table F[41]

F4   VARIATION OF PROFIT SHARES AND DRAWINGS
            The Partners shall review the division of profits and losses in every [third]
            Accounting Period[42] the first such review to take place in the Accounting
            Period commencing the [. . .] day of [. . .] 199[. . .] and shall review
            the amount of monthly drawings in every [third] Accounting Period in
            each case by the [end of the first month] in the relevant Accounting Period
            and shall Resolve upon the changes to such shares and drawings to have
            effect in respect of that Accounting Period. Upon the passing of such
            Resolution Table F shall be amended accordingly and initialled by [the
            Senior Partner or the Managing Partner][43]

---

[40]   In most businesses, there can be problems about occasional income earned by partners which may be
       seen as being related to the firm. I recommend that this issue should be addressed in the Agreement.
       These examples are appropriate to solicitors.
[41]   It is a good discipline to establish fixed drawing limits for partners as a protection against overdrawing.
       In the absence of agreement, partners are not allowed drawings until after the signature of the
       partnership accounts.
[42]   There will be many variations of this clause. Whilst there are different approaches to profit division,
       firms adopt in general five different methods of varying profits:
       1   'Equality'   All partners are equal.
       2   'Lock step'   Partners progress by a number of predetermined steps to equality.
       3   'Dead men's shoes'   Changes in partnership shares take place on retirement or death by the
                                 remaining partners succeeding pro-rata to the departing partner's share.
       4   'Renegotiation'   The partners renegotiate shares at preset intervals.
       5   'Certification'   A committee of the partners (usually elected) certifies variations in profit
                                 shares – sometimes against preset criteria.
       This is a precedent for the renegotiation method.
[43]   See Clause 10.5 at p 31.

F5   ANNUAL ACCOUNTS
F5.1   The Annual Accounts shall be prepared as soon as practical after each
            Accounting Date by reference to generally accepted accounting princi-
            ples

F5.2   The profits shall be calculated after making provision for interest on
            Advances (if any) and the salary payable to any salaried partner[44] arising
            during the Accounting Period and the balance sheet shall comprise the
            assets of the Partnership normally included in a balance sheet

F5.3   The Annual Accounts shall be agreed to by a Resolution of the Partners
            and signed by all the Partners or by the Partner or Partners nominated for
            that purpose in the Resolution. When so signed the Annual Accounts shall
            be binding on all the Partners except that if any manifest error therein be
            detected within 6 months after such signature such error shall be rectified
            immediately

F5.4   The Annual Accounts shall be prepared on the basis that (unless otherwise
            Resolved)[45]:
            F5.4.1   the goodwill of the Partnership shall be treated as having no value
                      and the value thereof (if any) shall not feature therein
            F5.4.2   the written down value of any fixed asset shall not be increased
            F5.4.3   the Annual Accounts for each Accounting Period shall be
                      prepared on a consistent basis with the previous Annual Accounts
                      (if any)

F6   DISTRIBUTION OF PROFITS
F6.1   The profits of the Partnership in each Accounting Period after taking into
            account drawings and such reserves as shall be Resolved upon by the
            Partners [on the advice of the Partnership Accountants][46] (including the
            reserves referred to in Clause F8.1) shall be divided between the Partners
            immediately after they have signed the Annual Accounts in respect of that
            Accounting Period[47]

F6.2   If it shall appear at any time that any Partner has drawn out more than the
            amount of drawings authorised pursuant to Clause F3 or more than his or
            her profit share in respect of any Accounting Period that Partner shall
            forthwith repay the deficiency to the Partnership and until such repayment
            the amount of such deficiency shall be a first charge on and be set off

---

[44]   See Clause 3.3 at p 26.
[45]   See note 77 below.
[46]   Clearly, advice will be taken from the partnership accountants in relation to tax reserves, but this
       clause is a reminder that other reserves may cause some contention between partners – eg a sinking
       fund for building refurbishment or purchase. This issue should be considered in connection with
       Clause F1.1, as a permanent requirement for reserve should be dealt with as an increase in capital.
       This clause *obliges* the partners to obtain advice from the accountants, which can take the heat out
       of the argument.
[47]   A reminder that partners are entitled to draw their surplus profits after signature of the accounts. If
       the partnership cannot afford a run on its bank account, then the partners should decide to reserve
       or increase capital. And see Clause F7 at p 38 as to advances.

against future drawings [and shall bear interest at [2 per cent per annum over the base rate for the time being of the Firm's bankers calculated with 3-monthly rests][48] from the last day of that Accounting Period until repayment][49]

F7   ADVANCES[50]
F7.1   If after the signature of any Annual Accounts any Partner shall elect not to withdraw any part of the accrued profit share to which he or she is then entitled to withdraw the amount not so withdrawn (if in excess of [£5,000]) shall be deemed to be an advance to the Partnership and shall carry interest at [the base rate for the time being of the Firm's bankers calculated with 3-monthly rests][51] from the date of signature[52] of such Annual Accounts until withdrawal (or at such other rate and on such other basis as may be determined by a Resolution of the Partners)

F7.2   Any Partner shall be entitled to withdraw any Advance at any time save that 28 days' notice shall be given to the other Partners prior to making a withdrawal (or total withdrawals in any period of 3 months) in excess of [£25,000]

F8   TAXATION[53]
F8.1   In respect of each Accounting Period [to which Section 215 of the Finance Act 1994 applies] the Partners shall Resolve upon the amount of income tax which they estimate [on the advice of the Partnership Accountants][54] to be payable by each Partner in respect of such period[55]

---

[48]   The rate at which the firm borrows money from its bank would seem appropriate.

[49]   As partners are not normally entitled to interest on capital (see note 34 above), it may be appropriate to charge interest to overdrawn partners.

[50]   Advances made by payment to the firm of cash (as opposed to advances made by not withdrawing profit share) are entitled to interest at 5% (Partnership Act 1890, s 24(3)). If a partner is prepared to advance cash, interest arrangements should be negotiated at the time of the credit.

[51]   A rate should be selected which encourages partners to leave capital with the firm and which has some advantage to the firm as well. Base rate seems appropriate.

[52]   I suggest that it is equitable for a partner making an advance not to receive interest until the accounts are signed (because he or she has no choice until such signature) and it is also fair to charge overdrawn partners with interest from the accounting date (because drawings are a privilege not a right).

[53]   This clause is drafted to deal with both the new tax rules for partnerships under the Finance Act 1994, s 215 (replacing the Income and Corporation Taxes Act 1988, s 111) (see Appendix) and also firms which still have the opportunity to make a continuation election under the old Income and Corporation Taxes Act 1988, s 113. (These are firms which commenced trade before 6 April 1994 and which have not decided to adopt an actual basis of taxation.) For firms which are on the new basis at the time of signature of the Agreement and which have no 'open' years on the old basis, the words in brackets in the first two lines of Clause F8.1 and Clauses F8.2 to F8.5 can be deleted. See heading 'Taxation' in 'About the Law' in the Introduction.

[54]   See note 46 above.

[55]   Even though the partners have no joint liability for income tax under the new rules, it is considered desirable not to permit partners to draw against profits on the basis that they will settle their own tax when the bill arrives. For some partners, the temptation to spend the apparent extra income may be difficult to resist. Most existing firms already reserve for tax and most existing partners will be prepared to accept a continuation of present practice. In most firms, the partnership accountants will continue to prepare the tax computations.

and which they shall transfer to Tax Reserve in respect of each Partner. Each such reserve shall be retained until an assessment to income tax is made upon the relevant Partner and the amount of the assessment (or so much thereof as is represented by the reserve) shall be paid to H.M. Collector of Taxes on the date when the assessment is due for payment. Any surplus of the reserve made in respect of that assessment shall thereupon be repaid to the relevant Partner and any deficiency shall be provided by the relevant Partner out of his or her own resources. Such reserves shall not constitute Advances but shall carry interest at the rate set out in Clause F7.1 from the date of the Resolution until payment

F8.2   Upon or after any Partner ceasing to be a Partner and upon or after the admission of any new Partner all Partners (including a new Partner and any former Partner and the personal representatives of any deceased Partner) shall if so Resolved by the Partners join in giving to H.M. Inspector of Taxes or any other requisite authority in such form as may be required any notice and join in making any election or the withdrawal or amendment thereof relating to any fiscal matter in connection with the affairs of the Partnership and for this purpose shall sign any such document and do any such act and provide any such information as shall be necessary to give effect to such Resolution. The Partners may Resolve to nominate a Partner to sign such document on behalf of some or all of the Partners[56]

F8.3   The Partners shall indemnify any former Partner and his or her estate and effects from and against any taxation of whatsoever nature suffered by him or her or his or her estate as a result of ceasing to be a Partner in excess of what would have been suffered by such former Partner or his or her estate and effects had such notice or election or withdrawal or amendment thereof (as the case may be) not been given

[F8.4   The Partners (other than the new Partner to whom the indemnity is given) shall indemnify any new Partner from and against any taxation of whatsoever nature suffered in excess of what would have been suffered by such new Partner as a result of his or her admission as a Partner had such notice or election or withdrawal or amendment thereof (as the case may be) not been given][57]

F8.5   Each Partner hereby appoints as his or her attorney so far as he or she may lawfully do so a Partner nominated by the Resolution pursuant to Clause

---

[56]   Under the 'old' regime, unless an election is made under the Income and Corporation Taxes Act 1988, s 113 the firm has a 'cessation' for tax purposes on a partner leaving or joining the firm. A cessation is the 'default' position and so the indemnity is given if there is a continuation. However, if profits are reducing, a partner who leaves may have an additional tax liability if no election to continue is made.

[57]   Many firms do not consider it appropriate to give this indemnity to an incoming partner.

F8.2 in his or her name and on his or her behalf to sign any such document as aforesaid[58]

F9   BOOKS OF ACCOUNT

F9.1   All proper and usual books of account and entries therein shall be kept (in either paper or electronic form) by the Partners and each Partner shall ensure that full and proper entries are duly and punctually made of all business transacted by him or her or at his or her direction on account of the Firm

F9.2   Each Partner and his or her agent or agents and the Partnership Accountants shall have access to the said books at all times and shall be entitled to make copies thereof or extracts therefrom as they shall respectively think fit

F10   BANKING

F10.1   The Firm shall maintain bank accounts with such bankers as the Partners shall from time to time Resolve

F10.2   All Partnership monies (not required for current expenses) and securities for monies shall as and when received be paid into or deposited with the Firm's bankers for the credit of the Firm's accounts. All cheques on such accounts shall be drawn by any [one] Partner in respect of amounts under [£1,000] for any one payee and by any [2] Partners in respect of amounts of [£1,000] or over unless otherwise Resolved by the Partners

F10.3   No Partner shall be entitled to open any Firm's bank account without the prior consent of [the Managing Partner] or not less than 2 of the other Partners

---

[58] There is no authority for an agent to sign a tax election, except under power of attorney. This is one reason for executing the Agreement under seal.

TABLE F[59]

Capital Contributions Profit Shares and Drawings

Capital contributions[60] profit shares[61] and drawings[62] with effect from the [. . .] day of [. . .] 199[. . .] shall be as follows:

Partner	Capital	Profit share[63]	Monthly drawings
[name (1)]	£	[. . .]%	£
[name (2)]	£	[. . .]%	£
[name (3)]	£	[. . .]%	£
[name (4)]	£	[. . .]%	£
Total	£	100%	£

---

[59] Tables are placed on separate pages for ease of replacement. See Clause 10.5 and note 26 at p 31.

[60] See Clause F1 at p 35.

[61] See Clause F2 at p 35.

[62] See Clause F3 at p 36.

[63] Percentage or points? Many larger firms prefer a points system for the following reasons:

   1 It avoids calculating shares to several decimal points.

   2 Partners do not feel that they have 'given up' something when a new partner is admitted. Each partner's number of points can remain the same; but the total number increases.

   3 If a partner leaves, his or her shares can be cancelled.

   4 It gives easy flexibility to award partners who perform well some bonus points in one year.

SCHEDULE I

Interpretation and Definitions

I1   DEFINITIONS
In this Agreement the following expressions shall where the context so admits have the following meanings:

'Accounting Date'	the date up to which the Annual Accounts are drawn and until otherwise Resolved[64] the [...] day of [...] in each year
'Accounting Period'	the period from one Accounting Date to the next Accounting Date
'Advance'	an advance by a Partner in accordance with Clause F7
'Annual Accounts'	the accounts drawn in accordance with Schedule F
'Capital Account'	in relation to any Partner his or her share of the capital of the Partnership in accordance with Clause F1
'Eligible Votes'[65]	the votes of all Partners [whether or not attending a meeting *or* attending a meeting *or* including votes by proxy in accordance with Clause M2.2] except a Partner disqualified from voting pursuant to Clause M3
'Firm'	the business carried on by the Partners in partnership under the Firm Name pursuant to this Agreement

---

[64] 'Resolve' and 'Resolution' are defined terms. See definitions in this Schedule and Table M at p 47.

[65] This definition needs careful consideration. Is voting by.

   1   all partners?; or
   2   all partners who attend a meeting?;
   3   counting proxy votes (if allowed)?; and
   4   votes by percentage of capital or votes allocated per partner? (For an example of allocation, see Precedent 4: Trading Firm Partnership Agreement, Clause M2.1 at p 131 and Schedule P at p 135).

   Considerations of quorum (Clause M2) are also important as the firm may not wish to enable one or two partners to prevent decisions being made by not attending meetings.

'Firm Name'	[*X Y and Z*] or any colourable imitation thereof or any combination of names which include any or all of [*X Y or Z*] or any colourable imitation of any such respective names
'Managing Partner'	the Partner elected in accordance with Clause M6
'Partners'	the persons whose names are set out in Schedule P and where the context so admits such of them as shall continue to be Partners in the Partnership and any other future Partners for the time being but not any salaried partners
'the Partnership'	the partnership [presently subsisting *or* created hereby] between the Partners including any partnership which is a successor to that partnership under whatever name
'Partnership Accountants'	Messrs [. . .] or such other chartered accountants as the Partners shall Resolve
'Resolve' and 'Resolution'	to determine in accordance with Schedule M
'Retirement Capital'[66]	a sum equal to the amount of capital standing to the credit of a Partner in his or her Capital Account on his or her Termination Date after deducting therefrom

    1. (if the Partner shall have been expelled from the Partnership pursuant to Clause T7) such sum as the remaining Partners shall Resolve to be necessary or sufficient to discharge all or any liability of the Partnership directly or indirectly attributable to the conduct of the Partner

    [2. such sum as [in the opinion of the Partnership Accountants *or* Senior Partner] may be required to satisfy his or her share of any income tax assessment which may be made upon the Partnership for any year of assessment

---

[66]   See note 83 below.

	ended prior to his or her Termination Date; and

3. the appropriate proportion of his or her share of any income tax assessment which may be made upon the Partnership for the year of assessment in which he or she ceases to be a Partner][67]

'Retirement Interest'   interest at [. . . per cent per annum above the base rate of [. . .] Bank plc from time to time] computed with [6-monthly] rests[68]

'Senior Partner'   the Partner elected in accordance with Clause M5

'Table F'   the table at the end of Schedule F

'Table M'   the table at the end of Schedule M

'Tax Reserve'   the amount standing to the credit of a Partner in the books of the Partnership for that Partner's reserve for taxation pursuant to Clause F8.1

'Termination Date'   the date on which a Partner ceases to be a Partner whether pursuant to this Agreement or by death

I2   INTERPRETATION

I2.1   Headings to Clauses and Schedules are for ease of reference only and shall be of no effect in construing the provisions of this Agreement

I2.2   Where the context so admits:

    I2.2.1   words importing the singular number shall include the plural and words importing the plural number shall include the singular

    I2.2.2   references to statutes or to sections of statutes shall include any statutory modifications or re-enactments thereof for the time being in force

---

[67] For firms which are on the new tax rules for partnerships under the Finance Act 1994, s 215 (replacing the Income and Corporation Taxes Act 1988, s 111) (see Appendix) at the time of signature of the Agreement and which have no 'open' years on the old basis, the words in brackets can be deleted. See note 53 above.

[68] The interest rate could be the same as the rate at which the firm borrows funds from its bankers. There is no reason for the firm to profit from the capital of a retired partner, although its retention will help cash flow.

SCHEDULE M

Meetings – Voting and Management

M1   PARTNERS MEETINGS
            The Partners shall meet for the purpose of dealing with Partnership
            matters at times and dates of which at least [one week's][69] notice shall be
            given by any Partner to all Partners (except in case of emergency)

M2   QUORUM [AND PROXY APPOINTMENT]
M2.1   The quorum for Partnership meetings shall be [all *or* all but one *or* *number*]
            of the Partners personally present [at the commencement of *or* through-
            out] the meeting

[M2.2   A Partner who is unable to attend the meeting for good cause may (subject
            to Clause M3) appoint another Partner his or her proxy to vote on his or
            her behalf in respect of any business to be transacted at the meeting [the
            topic of which has been notified to that Partner before the meeting]. Any
            appointment of a proxy shall be in writing, and unless otherwise instructed
            the proxy may vote as he or she thinks fit or abstain from voting][70]

M3   VOTING RESTRICTIONS
            A Partner shall not be entitled to vote [personally or by proxy] on a
            Resolution[71]:

M3.1   for his or her election as Senior Partner pursuant to Clause M5

M3.2   for his or her election as Managing Partner pursuant to Clause M6

M3.3   to cause his or her retirement by reason of incapacity pursuant to Clause
            T6

M3.4   to expel him or her pursuant to Clause T7

M3.5   to cause his or her compulsory retirement pursuant to Clause T8

M3.6   to suspend him or her pursuant to Clause T9

M4   VOTING PERCENTAGES
M4.1   For a Resolution to be passed arising under the Clause set out in column
            1 of Table M a brief description of which (for convenience and not by way

---

[69]   The period and formalities of notice will vary according to the size of the firm and the location of
       its offices.
[70]   Partners tend to have strongly divided views as to the desirability of proxy voting. Such a provision
       is desirable in larger firms, and important if a very high percentage is adopted for quorum in Clause
       M2.1 to avoid inquorate meetings.
[71]   'Resolve' and 'Resolution' are defined terms. See definitions in Schedule I at p 43 and Table M at
       p 47.

of construction) is set out in column 2 of Table M the percentage of Eligible Votes[72] set out in column 3 of Table M must be in favour of the Resolution

M4.2   All decisions of the Partners which do not arise under any Clause shall be made by Resolution

[M5   SENIOR PARTNER
           The Partners (excluding the Partner proposed for election) may Resolve that a Partner be elected to the office of Senior Partner. Such Partner shall be elected for a term of 3 years and may be re-elected [once]. The Senior Partner at the date hereof is [*name*] whose term of office expires on [. . .] and who is [not] eligible for re-election][73]

[M6   MANAGING PARTNER
           The Partners (excluding the Partner proposed for election) may Resolve that a Partner be elected to the office of Managing Partner. Such Partner shall be elected for a term of 3 years and may be re-elected [once]. The Managing Partner at the date hereof is [*name*] whose term of office expires on [. . .] and who is [not] eligible for re-election][74]

---

[72] Careful consideration needs to be given to this definition. See note 65 above.
[73] See note 74 below.
[74] In many firms, such formal arrangements are inappropriate. The clauses do not indicate the authority of a senior or managing partner; indeed, as drafted, no authority is delegated. Delegation is best left to partners' resolutions, except for larger firms, which might wish to expand these clauses to provide for election of a management committee and real delegation of authority. For example, any decision of the partners which requires a simple majority of the partners could be delegated to a unanimous decision of a management committee. For an example of delegation, see Precedent 4: Trading Firm Partnership Agreement, Clause M4 at p 131.

TABLE M[75]

Voting Percentages

Clause	Brief description	Percentage of Eligible Votes[76]
2.2	Change Firm Name	[51]
3.1	Admit new Partner	[100]
3.2	Agree merger	[100]
3.3	Appoint salaried Partner	[75]
5.1	Change Partnership premises	[75]
6.1	Change holiday entitlement	[51]
7.1	Change pension provision	[75]
7.2	Change personal insurances	[75]
8	Waive restrictions	[75]
8.4	Not to act for client	[51]
8.5	Adopt unauthorised expenditure	[51]
10.1	Vary Agreement – financial/voting	[100]
10.2	Vary Agreement – other	[51]
10.6	Variations of Agreement for individual Partners	The percentage applicable to the Clause varied
D1	Dissolve Partnership	[100]
F1.1	Fix Partnership capital	[100]
F4	Review profit shares	[100]

[75] Tables are placed on separate pages for ease of replacement. See Clause 10.5 and note 26 at p 31.
[76] See note 65 above and Clause M4 at p 45. All of the percentages in this Table are merely suggestions.

Clause		Brief description	Percentage of Eligible Votes
F4		Review drawings	[100]
F5.3		Agree Annual Accounts	[75]
F5.4		Change accounting basis[77]	[100]
F6.1		Agree reserves	[75]
F7.1		Vary interest on Advances	[75]
F8.1		Estimate Tax Reserves	[75]
F8.2		Sign tax election	[75]
F10.1		Change bank	[51]
F10.2		Change bank mandate	[51]
I1		Change Accounting Date[78]	[100]
I1		Change Partnership Accountants	[51]
I1		Reserve from expelled Partner	[51]
M4.2		Resolution not varying the Agreement	[51]
M5	★	Elect Senior Partner	[51]
M6	★	Elect Managing Partner	[51]
T6.1	★	Retire Partner for incapacity	[100]
T7.1	★	Expel Partner	[100]
T8.1	★	Retire Partner compulsorily	[100]
T9.1	★	Suspend Partner	[100]

★ Clause M3 restricts entitlement to vote on these Resolutions

---

[77] This resolution should require the same number of votes as the resolution to change profit shares (Clause F4) as it may well have the effect of penalising a partner on changes in shares, or retirement. For example, a decision in a professional firm to change the basis on which work in progress is valued (or in a trading company to change the basis of stock valuation), or to change the basis of depreciation, will have the effect of altering the profits which arise in that accounting period.

[78] 100% is suggested for changing the accounting date as it may have implications for profit shares (if shares change at the end of an accounting period), and also for the retirement date under Clause T4 and T5.1.

SCHEDULE P

The Partners

Name and address	Identifying initials	Date joined	Date ceased

SCHEDULE R[79]

Repayment Arrangements[80] on Termination[81]
This Schedule does not have effect on Dissolution[82]

R1   RETIRING PARTNER
            If any Partner shall retire pursuant to Clause T4.1[83]

R1.1   any Advance made by him or her together with all accrued interest at his
            or her Termination Date shall be repaid to him or her or his or her
            personal representatives within [3] months from his or her Termination
            Date

[R1.2   any Tax Reserve held for him or her together with all accrued interest at
            his or her Termination Date shall be repaid to him or her or his or her
            personal representatives within [3] months from his or her Termination
            Date]

R1.3   a payment on account of his or her profit share from the previous
            Accounting Date until his or her Termination Date shall be paid to him or

[79] This Schedule sets out the repayment arrangements to partners who have left for one of six different
      reasons:
      1 Retirement
      2 Resignation
      3 Incapacity
      4 Expulsion
      5 Compulsory retirement; and
      6 Death.
      Six separate clauses have been drafted to allow for different capital repayment time-tables, and
      different payments of interest. In practice, most firms will adopt the same repayment arrangements
      for most circumstances and some or all of Clauses R1 to R6 can be combined.
[80] Schedule T deals with steps leading to termination (notice periods etc) and this Schedule deals with
      the payment arrangements consequent upon termination.
[81] This precedent contains no provision for payment for goodwill or payments of pensions to former
      partners, as such provisions are effectively obsolete in professional firms. For an example, see
      Precedent 4: Trading Firm Partnership Agreement, Clause T5 at p 139.
[82] This Schedule does not have effect if, following termination, there is only one partner. See Clause
      D1 at p 33.
[83] Payments on retirement consist of five elements:
      1 Repayment of Advances (see Clause F7 at p 38).
      2 Repayment of Tax Reserve (see Clause F8.1 at p 38).
      3 Profit share from the last Accounting Date to the Retirement Date.
      4 Retirement Capital (see definition in Schedule I at p 43).
      5 Retirement Interest (see definition in Schedule I at p 44).
      These may be paid by the same or different instalments. If items 1 to 4 are all to be paid by the same
      instalments then the definition of Retirement Capital in Schedule I can be expanded to include all
      four, and this and the succeeding clauses shortened accordingly.

her or his or her personal representatives within [3] months from his or her Termination Date and the balance thereof as soon as the Annual Accounts for the Accounting Period ending on the Termination Date (if the Termination Date shall be an Accounting Date) or next following the Termination Date (as the case may be) shall have been signed by the Partners in accordance with Clause F5.3

R1.4   the Retirement Capital of such Partner shall be repaid to him or her by [6] equal [6-monthly] instalments the first of such instalments to be paid to him or her [6] months after his or her Termination Date

R1.5   Retirement Interest calculated from the Termination Date shall be paid with each payment of his or her Advance [and his or her Tax Reserve] (including accrued interest to his or her Termination Date) his or her profit share and his or her Retirement Capital

R2   **RESIGNING PARTNER**
If any Partner shall resign pursuant to Clause T5.1[84]

R2.1   any Advance made by him or her together with all accrued interest at his or her Termination Date shall be repaid to him or her or his or her personal representatives within [3] months from his or her Termination Date

[R2.2   any Tax Reserve held for him or her together with all accrued interest at his or her Termination Date shall be repaid to him or her or his or her personal representatives within [3] months from his or her Termination Date]

R2.3   a payment on account of his or her profit share from the previous Accounting Date until his or her Termination Date shall be paid to him or her or his or her personal representatives within [3] months from his or her Termination Date and the balance thereof as soon as the Annual Accounts for the Accounting Period ending on the Termination Date (if the Termination Date shall be an Accounting Date) or next following the Termination Date (as the case may be) shall have been signed by the Partners in accordance with Clause F5.3

R2.4   the Retirement Capital of such Partner shall be repaid to him or her by [6] equal [6-monthly] instalments the first of such instalments to be paid to him or her [6] months after his or her Termination Date[85]

R2.5   Retirement Interest calculated from the Termination Date shall be paid with each payment of his or her Advance [and his or her Tax Reserve] (including accrued interest to his or her Termination Date) his or her profit share and his or her Retirement Capital

---

[84]   See note 83 above.
[85]   Some firms delay repayment of capital to partners who resign with a view to working elsewhere.

R3   INCAPACITATED PARTNER
            In the event of the retirement of any Partner by reason of incapacity
            pursuant to Clause T6[86]

R3.1   any Advance made by him or her together with all accrued interest at his
            or her Termination Date shall be repaid to him or her or his or her
            personal representatives within [3] months from his or her Termination
            Date

[R3.2   any Tax Reserve held for him or her together with all accrued interest at
            his or her Termination Date shall be repaid to him or her or his or her
            personal representatives within [3] months from his or her Termination
            Date]

R3.3   a payment on account of his or her profit share from the previous
            Accounting Date until his or her Termination Date shall be paid to him or
            her or his or her personal representatives within [3] months from his or her
            Termination Date and the balance thereof as soon as the Annual Accounts
            for the Accounting Period ending on the Termination Date (if the
            Termination Date shall be an Accounting Date) or next following the
            Termination Date (as the case may be) shall have been signed by the
            Partners in accordance with Clause F5.3

R3.4   the Retirement Capital of such Partner shall be repaid to him or her by [6]
            equal [6-monthly] instalments the first of such instalments to be paid to
            him or her [6] months after his or her Termination Date[87]

R3.5   Retirement Interest calculated from the Termination Date shall be paid
            with each payment of his or her Advance [and his or her Tax Reserve]
            (including accrued interest to his or her Termination Date) his or her
            profit share and his or her Retirement Capital

R4   EXPELLED PARTNER
            In the event of the expulsion of any Partner pursuant to Clause T7[88]

R4.1   any Advance made by him or her together with all accrued interest at his
            or her Termination Date shall be repaid to him or her or his or her
            personal representatives within [12] months from his or her Termination
            Date

[R4.2   any Tax Reserve held for him or her together with all accrued interest at
            his or her Termination Date shall be repaid to him or her or his or her
            personal representatives within [3] months from his or her Termination
            Date]

R4.3   a payment on account of his or her profit share from the previous
            Accounting Date until his or her Termination Date shall be paid to him or

---

[86] See note 83 above.
[87] It is common practice to accelerate payments to incapacitated partners.
[88] See note 83 above.

her or his or her personal representatives within [12] months from his or her Termination Date and the balance thereof [within [6] months after] the Annual Accounts for the Accounting Period ending on the Termination Date (if the Termination Date shall be an Accounting Date) or next following the Termination Date (as the case may be) shall have been signed by the Partners in accordance with Clause F5.3

R4.4   the Retirement Capital of such Partner shall be repaid to him or her by [6] equal [annual] instalments the first of such instalments to be paid to him or her [12] months after his or her Termination Date

R4.5   [Retirement Interest calculated from the Termination Date shall be paid with each payment of his or her Advance [and his or her Tax Reserve] (including accrued interest to his or her Termination Date) his or her profit share and his or her Retirement Capital *or* no Retirement Interest shall be paid][89]

R5   COMPULSORY RETIREMENT
In the event of the compulsory retirement of any Partner pursuant to Clause T8[90]

R5.1   any Advance made by him or her together with all accrued interest at his or her Termination Date shall be repaid to him or her or his or her personal representatives within [3] months from his or her Termination Date

[R5.2   any Tax Reserve held for him or her together with all accrued interest at his or her Termination Date shall be repaid to him or her or his or her personal representatives within [3] months from his or her Termination Date]

R5.3   a payment on account of his or her profit share from the previous Accounting Date until his or her Termination Date shall be paid to him or her or his or her personal representatives within [3] months from his or her Termination Date and the balance thereof as soon as the Annual Accounts for the Accounting Period ending on the Termination Date (if the Termination Date shall be an Accounting Date) or next following the Termination Date (as the case may be) shall have been signed by the Partners in accordance with Clause F5.3

[R5.4   if the Termination Date shall occur less than 6 months after the date of the Resolution[91] for his or her compulsory retirement there shall be credited to his or her Capital Account as soon as the same can be calculated a sum of money which together with his or her profit share from the date of the Resolution for his or her compulsory retirement shall be equal to one half

---

[89]   Some firms both delay payment and withhold (or do not pay) interest for expelled partners.
[90]   See note 83 above.
[91]   'Resolve' and 'Resolution' are defined terms. See definitions in Schedule I at p 43 and Table M at p 47.

of his or her profit share during the Accounting Period ending prior to the date of the Resolution][92]

R5.5　　　the Retirement Capital of such Partner shall be repaid to him or her by [6] equal [6-monthly] instalments the first of such instalments to be paid to him or her [6] months after his or her Termination Date

R5.6　　　Retirement Interest calculated from the Termination Date shall be paid with each payment of his or her Advance [and his or her Tax Reserve] (including accrued interest to his or her Termination Date) his or her profit share and his or her Retirement Capital

R6　　　　DECEASED PARTNER
In the event of the death of any Partner whilst a Partner[93]

R6.1　　　any Advance made by him or her together with all accrued interest at his or her death shall be repaid to his or her personal representatives within [3] months from the date of his or her death

[R6.2　　any Tax Reserve held for him or her together with all accrued interest at his or her death shall be repaid to his or her personal representatives within [3] months from the date of his or her death]

R6.3　　　a payment on account of his or her profit share from the previous Accounting Date until the date of his or her death shall be paid to his or her personal representatives within [3 months] from such date and the balance thereof as soon as the Annual Accounts for the Accounting Period next following such date shall have been signed by the Partners in accordance with Clause F5.3

R6.4　　　the Retirement Capital of such Partner shall be repaid to his or her personal representatives by [6] equal [6-monthly] instalments the first of such instalments to be paid to his or her personal representatives [6] months after the date of his or her death

R6.5　　　Retirement Interest calculated from his or her death shall be paid with each payment of his or her Advance [and his or her Tax Reserve] (including accrued interest to the date of his or her death) his or her profit share and his or her Retirement Capital

R7　　　　ALL PAYMENTS
R7.1　　　Sums retained from Retirement Capital for income tax which are not required to satisfy a Partner's share of any income tax assessments which may be made upon the Partnership shall be credited to the Partner's Retirement Capital (or paid to him or her if his or her Retirement Capital has been repaid) as soon as the relevant income tax assessment has been agreed with the Inland Revenue and any deficiency in any sum so retained shall be reimbursed by the Partner on demand

---

[92]　It is recommended that partners subject to compulsory retirement (as to which see note 106 below) should be given enhanced payment on termination.
[93]　See note 83 above.

R7.2   If at the date that payment of any instalment of Retirement Capital or
          Retirement Interest is due the amount of such payment has not been
          ascertained then a reasonable amount on account of such payment shall be
          made on such date and the remainder of such payment shall be made as
          soon as the same shall have been ascertained

R8   PROVISIONS APPLICABLE ON THE DEATH OF A FORMER
          PARTNER
          Sums due to a former Partner who has ceased to be a Partner prior to his
          or her death shall continue to be paid to his or her personal representatives
          in the same manner as they would have been paid to him or her had he or
          she not died

Practical Partnership Agreements

SCHEDULE T

Termination and Suspension Provisions

This Schedule shall not have effect if, following termination, there shall be only one Partner

T1   GENERAL PROVISIONS

T1.1   The following provisions of this Clause shall apply in the event of a Partner ceasing to be a Partner unless there shall then remain only one Partner (in which event Schedule D shall have effect)[94]

T1.2   Upon a Partner ceasing to be a Partner his or her profit share shown in Table F shall be cancelled and the amounts due to him or her shall be repaid in accordance with Schedule R

T1.3   The remaining Partners shall succeed to all the interest of the former Partner in the Partnership (subject to his or her rights herein contained) [in the shares which as between themselves they share profits *or* equally][95] and shall undertake all the debts liabilities and obligations of the former Partner and will indemnify and keep the former Partner indemnified against all such debts liabilities and obligations other than such as are hereby deemed to be for his or her separate account or are directly or indirectly attributable to any act or omission of the former Partner but without prejudice to any subsisting liability of the former Partner for breach of this Agreement[96]

---

[94]   If it is likely that the firm may reduce to only two or three partners consider using Precedent 2: Small Firm Partnership Agreement or adapting Clause T4 (and related clauses) from it dealing with succession in these circumstances.

[95]   Careful consideration needs to be given to this issue. Allocating a share equally between the remaining partners can help in a move towards equality of shares. If a points system is used, it may be sufficient merely to say that points are cancelled.

[96]   This clause can give rise to many difficulties.

    First, it must be made clear that a partner will not be indemnified against his or her own default. So a partner who is expelled for cause remains liable to indemnify his former partners against loss arising from that default.

    Second, a partner who is negligent remains liable to indemnify for his or her own negligence. This is not an issue if the firm has sufficient negligence insurance to cover a claim, as the insurance extends to all partners, including one who is negligent. Moreover, in most cases of negligence, the claim rarely arises exclusively from one person's mistake, making claims difficult to pursue inside a firm.

    Third is the liability of all partners for negligence claims in excess of the firm's insurance cover. My view is that if such a claim has been intimated at the termination date, a reserve should be included in the retirement accounts, but if not the former partner should get a full indemnity against future claims, whenever the negligent act happened.

T1.4   If and so far as it shall be necessary to apportion profits and losses for any period the apportionment shall be on a time basis by reference to the then current Accounting Period

T1.5   If any Partner (including a former Partner) so requires due notice of the fact of the former Partner leaving the Partnership shall be given by advertisement in the London Gazette and each Partner including a former Partner shall sign and concur in all necessary or proper notices for that purpose and on any Partner or a former Partner refusing or failing to do so any other Partner may sign the name of such Partner to any such notice

T1.6   A former Partner shall have no rights whatsoever against any remaining Partner save as herein expressly provided

T2   RESTRICTIONS[97]

A former Partner [other than a Partner who is subject to compulsory retirement pursuant to Clause T8][98] shall not:

T2.1   at any time solicit whether by himself or herself or as a partner or employee of any other person firm or company directly or indirectly any person firm or company who shall have been a client of the Firm [other than a client personally introduced by him or her to the Firm[99] and other than his or her relatives or a company wholly owned or controlled by him or her or his or her relatives] at any time during a period of 3 years immediately preceding the date when he or she ceased to be a Partner

T2.2   for a period of 3 years from the date of ceasing to be a Partner act as a [*occupation*] for any such client in manner aforesaid

T2.3   during a period of 3 years from the date of ceasing to be a Partner carry on or be concerned or engaged or interested whether directly or indirectly and whether by himself or herself or as a partner or employee of any other person firm or company in the [practice or profession of *or* business of . . .] within a radius of [one mile] from any address at which at the date of his or her ceasing to be a Partner the Firm shall be carrying on the Partnership business

T2.4   at any time after ceasing to be a Partner and in any place carry on business under any style or name which shall include or refer to the Firm Name

T2.5   at any time suggest or cause to be suggested to any member of the Firm's staff that he or she might leave the employment of the Firm to work for the former Partner or for any company or firm with which the former Partner is or intends to be connected

---

[97] These restrictions are by way of guidance only. Careful consideration must be given in each case having regard to the size of the firm, its business, its location and the other factors taken into account when considering the enforceability of restrictive covenants.

[98] It may be considered inappropriate to impose restrictive covenants on a partner who is subject to compulsory retirement. See also note 106 below.

[99] Disputes can arise over introductions of business unless the firm has a well-settled procedure for identifying introducers.

T2.6   at any time encourage or cause to be encouraged any such staff as aforesaid to leave the employment of the Firm to work as aforesaid

T3   SEVERANCE OF RESTRICTIONS
            It is hereby declared that the provisions of each of Clauses T2.1 to T2.6 respectively are intended to be read and construed independently of each other so that none of such separate provisions shall be dependent on any one or more of any of the other such provisions

T4   RETIREMENT BY AGE OR NOTICE
            Each Partner shall retire on the Accounting Date following his or her [65th] birthday and may (if he or she shall give to the other Partners not less than [6] months' notice in writing of his or her intention to do so) retire from the Partnership on any Accounting Date [after his or her 55th birthday][100]

T5   RESIGNATION[101]
T5.1   Any Partner may at any time give notice in writing to the other Partners of his or her desire to resign from the Partnership. Such notice shall in the absence of agreement to the contrary be of not less than [6] months expiring on any Accounting Date on or before his or her 55th birthday[102] and on the expiry of such notice such Partner shall cease to be a Partner

T5.2   If any Partner gives notice pursuant to Clause T5.1 (except where such notice has been given by reason of the permanent ill health of the Partner resigning) the remaining Partners shall each be entitled within 3 months thereafter themselves to give notice of retirement or resignation (as the case may be according to the age of the Partner giving such notice at the date of expiry of such notice) expiring on the same date as the original notice[103]

T6   RETIREMENT DUE TO INCAPACITY
T6.1   If a Partner has been or in the view of competent medical opinion is likely to be incapacitated from carrying out his or her duties as a Partner for the total period set out in Clause 6.2 (and without prejudice to the provisions of Clause 6.2) then the Partners may Resolve[104] that such Partner shall

---

[100]   See note 101 below.
[101]   This clause is only necessary if it is intended to impose different capital repayment arrangements for early retirees. If not, the whole of Clause T5.1 and the words in brackets at the end of the previous clause may be deleted. Consideration should then be given to incorporating Clause T5.2 into Clause T4.
[102]   See Clause T4 above.
[103]   This is only an appropriate clause for smaller firms, where the prospect of paying out a retiring partner could give rise to severe difficulties, particularly if the retiring partner is a major source of business introduction. This clause is included in the 'resignation' clause as it is considered that the retiring partner may be going to another firm. It is not appropriate to a retirement by age clause. In this case the retiring partner should have some assurance that he or she will get paid out.
[104]   'Resolve' and 'Resolution' are defined terms. See definitions in Schedule I at p 43 and Table M at p 47.

retire from the Partnership on the date specified in the Resolution by reason of incapacity in which event he or she shall cease to be a Partner on such date

T6.2 In relation hereto any two Partners may require any Partner to submit to an examination by a medical adviser nominated by such Partners

T7 EXPULSION

T7.1 If any Partner shall:

T7.1.1 charge assign or transfer his or her share in the Partnership or any part thereof or suffer the same to be charged for his or her separate debt under the Partnership Act 1890

T7.1.2 become bankrupt or insolvent or compound or make any arrangement with or for the benefit of his or her creditors or apply for an interim order pursuant to Section 253 of the Insolvency Act 1986 or have a petition for a bankruptcy order against him or her presented to the Court

T7.1.3 act in any manner inconsistent with the good faith observable between Partners

T7.1.4 be guilty of any conduct which would be a ground for dissolution of the Partnership by the Court

T7.1.5 absent himself or herself from the Partnership without proper cause for more than [4] weeks (consecutive or otherwise) in any period of 12 months[105]

T7.1.6 fail to comply with a requirement made under Clause T6.2

T7.1.7 be convicted of any offence involving fraud or dishonesty or be sentenced to a term of imprisonment whether or not suspended

T7.1.8 be suspended or expelled by the [*body*]

T7.1.9 be guilty of any flagrantly immoral behaviour or of any flagrant grave deliberate or persistent breach or breaches of the ethics or etiquette of the [. . .] profession or of any other conduct calculated or tending to injure the reputation of the Firm or likely to have a serious or adverse effect upon the Firm's business

T7.1.10 commit any substantial breach of this Agreement

then and in any such case the Partners may Resolve to determine the Partnership so far as it concerns such Partner on the date specified in the Resolution in which event he or she shall cease to be a Partner on such date and in such event the Partners may also Resolve either in the same or another Resolution that that Partner be suspended by being excluded from attending to the business and affairs of the Partnership from such date and for such period until the date of expulsion as may be specified in the Resolution

T7.2 If any question shall arise concerning the existence of the grounds for expulsion or exercise of the power to expel conferred by Clause T7.1 such

---

[105] Even 4 weeks may be too long for unexplained absences!

question shall be referred to arbitration under the provisions of Clause 11.2

T7.3   If following any such reference to arbitration it shall be determined that an alleged Partner remains or is entitled to remain a Partner then such Partner shall nevertheless be entitled to resign from the Partnership at any time within 21 days of receiving notification of such determination by giving to the other Partners or Partner notice in writing of his or her intention so to do and such retirement shall take effect for all purposes forthwith on the service of the said notice. No other Partner shall be entitled to give notice pursuant to Clause T5.2 in such event

T8   COMPULSORY RETIREMENT[106]

T8.1   Subject to the provisions of this Clause the Partners may Resolve that any Partner shall be compelled to retire from the Partnership without specifying any reason[107] with effect from the date specified in such Resolution in which event he or she shall cease to be a Partner on such date and in such event the Partners may also Resolve either in the same or another Resolution that that Partner be suspended by being excluded from attending to the business and affairs of the Partnership from such date and for such period until the date of retirement as may be specified in the Resolution

T8.2   A copy of the proposed Resolution for compulsory retirement shall be given to all Partners at least 28 days before the meeting at which the Resolution is to be proposed

T8.3   The provisions of this Clause shall only have effect if at the time of the Resolution set out in Clause T8.1 there shall be at least [4] Partners eligible to vote[108]

T9   SUSPENSION[109]

T9.1   Without prejudice to the power of expulsion conferred by Clause T7 and the power to bring about compulsory retirement conferred by Clause T8

---

[106] Compulsory retirement is intended to be used to remove a partner on a 'no fault' basis. For example, on an issue which requires a 100% vote of the partners (eg to increase the partnership capital), one partner may dissent from the view of the remainder. They may form the view that the objection by the one partner is inhibiting the progress of the firm. Indeed, it may have become a case of 'the tail wagging the dog', with the one partner demanding some benefit or concession as the price of agreement. The whole argument may arise over a genuine difference of view. In these circumstances, the remaining partners may conclude that compulsory retirement is the only method of resolving the issue.

    I do not recommend this clause at all for smaller firms (say four partners), as it could be used to take undue advantage of one partner. On the other hand, it is essential in firms which like to have 100% majorities on most issues. This is a Draconian right, and should only be exercised by a substantial majority of the remaining partners – at least 90% whatever the size of the firm. If the clause is used, it is appropriate to be more generous to such partners on retirement. See notes 92, 98 above.

[107] This is 'no fault' retirement – see note 106 above.

[108] See notes 106, 107 above, and Clause M4.1 at p 45 as to eligible votes.

[109] It may be considered that this power is inappropriate for small firms.

it shall be competent for the Partners to Resolve on one or more occasion without specifying any reason[110] that a Partner be suspended by being excluded from attending to the business and affairs of the Partnership from such date and for such period as may be specified in the Resolution not exceeding 6 weeks

T9.2 From the date specified in the Resolution the Partner concerned shall forthwith absent himself or herself from the premises and thereafter take no part in the business or affairs of the Partnership or its clients for the period of suspension. A suspended Partner shall not be entitled to attend or vote [(either in person or by proxy)] at any meeting of the Partners. Such suspension may be extended from time to time by further Resolutions as aforesaid

T9.3 During any period of suspension the Partner concerned shall continue to be entitled to his or her profit share and other rights of a Partner except as set out in Clause T9.2

T9.4 If within 21 days of the termination of such suspension no steps shall have been taken by the other Partners to expel or cause the compulsory retirement of the Partner who had been suspended such Partner shall nevertheless be entitled to resign from the Partnership at any time within the 21 days following such termination by giving to the other Partners or Partner notice in writing of his or her intention so to do and such retirement shall take effect for all purposes forthwith on the service of the said notice. No other Partner shall be entitled to give notice pursuant to Clause T5.2 in such event

T9.5 The provisions of this Clause shall only have effect if at the time of the Resolution set out in Clause T9.1 there shall be at least [4] Partners eligible to vote[111]

---

[110] It is inappropriate to specify a reason as this clause will normally be used when an expulsion is in contemplation, to allow for investigation. Bearing in mind the duty of good faith between partners, care should be used in exercising this power, as an unfair use could be grounds for dissolution by the court.

[111] See Clause M4.1 at p 45 as to eligible votes.

SCHEDULE V

Variations and Waivers Affecting Individual Partners[112]

(Clause 10.6)

---

[112] Insert here specific waivers given to individual partners, for example:

Time off or part-time work	Clause 4.2
Waivers re medical	Clause 6.4
Waivers re insurance	Clause 7
Waivers re outside directorships	Clause 8.1 etc.

SCHEDULE X

Execution

This Deed is intended to be delivered by each Partner on the date of delivery opposite that Partner's name

Name of Partner	*Signature as a Deed*	*Date of Delivery*	*Signature of Witness*
[*name (1)*]	....		....
[*name (2)*]	....		....
[*name (3)*]	....		....
[*name (4)*]	....		....

PRECEDENT 2:   SMALL FIRM PARTNERSHIP AGREEMENT FOR A PROFESSIONAL FIRM WITH OPTION FOR A SINGLE PARTNER TO CONTINUE

CONTENTS

PRECEDENT 2: SMALL FIRM PARTNERSHIP AGREEMENT FOR A PROFESSIONAL FIRM WITH OPTION FOR A SINGLE PARTNER TO CONTINUE[1]

THIS PARTNERSHIP AGREEMENT[2] executed as a Deed[3] constitutes the terms on which the Partners have agreed to carry on business in partnership as [*trade or profession*] and is intended to be known as

'THE [*name of firm*] 199[. . .] PARTNERSHIP AGREEMENT'[4]

1.   THE SCHEDULES
1.1   This Agreement includes the following Schedules and Tables:

Schedule D[5]	which contains **D**issolution provisions
Schedule F	which contains **F**inancial provisions
Table F	which contains details of capital profit shares and drawings
Schedule I	which contains **I**nterpretation of this Agreement and definitions used in this Agreement
Schedule M	which contains **M**eetings procedure and voting arrangements
Table M	which contains details of voting percentages
Schedule P	which contains **P**artners names and addresses
Schedule T	which contains **T**ermination and payment provisions
Schedule X	which contains e**X**ecution of this Agreement by the Partners

2.   DURATION – FIRM NAME
2.1   The Partnership shall continue until terminated in accordance with the provisions of this Agreement

---

[1] This precedent is a shorter form than Precedent 1: Standard Partnership Agreement suitable for up to about seven partners with options for a firm of two which intends to grow or a firm which might reduce to two partners.

[2] See 'About the Precedents' in the Introduction which describes the numbering system used in the documents. First-time users of this precedent should read Schedule I (Interpretation) first.

[3] The Agreement is executed as a deed (Schedule X) to give effect to the following clauses:

4.3	indemnity as to private debts;
5.2	trust of property (desirable not essential);
5.3	property indemnity;
F6.3 and F6.4	tax indemnities.

[4] As the Agreement may initially be executed by partners on different days, and subsequently amended and executed by new partners, it is identified by a name, and not dated. See 'About the Precedents' in the Introduction and the Partnership Act 1890, s 19 (see Appendix) as to variation of partnership deeds.

[5] See note 2 above.

2.2   The Partnership shall be carried on under the Firm Name or such other
           name or names as the Partners shall Resolve[6]

3.   CHANGES OF PARTNERS
3.1   No person shall be admitted as a Partner otherwise than by a Resolution
           of the Partners in favour of the introduction of the new Partner and the
           terms of the introduction

3.2   Any person becoming a Partner shall signify his or her acceptance of this
           Agreement by signing as a Deed in Schedule X opposite the entry of his
           or her name and his or her name address identifying initials and date of
           joining shall be inserted in Schedule P

3.3   If any Partner shall cease to be a Partner then the Partnership shall not be
           dissolved as to the other Partners [unless as a result thereof only one
           Partner remains in which event the Partnership shall be dissolved in
           accordance with Schedule D unless such Partner shall serve a Succession
           Notice][7]

3.4   There shall be inserted in Schedule P against the entry of the name of any
           person who has ceased to be a Partner the date upon which he or she so
           ceased

4.   GENERAL DUTIES OF THE PARTNERS
4.1   Each Partner shall be just and faithful to the other Partners in all
           transactions dealings and matters relating to or affecting the Partnership
           and shall in all circumstances give a true and proper account thereof when
           reasonably required so to do by any of the other Partners

4.2   Each Partner shall devote the whole of his or her time and attention to the
           business of the Firm and diligently and faithfully employ himself or herself
           therein and use his or her best endeavours to carry on the same for the
           utmost benefit of the Partnership[8]

4.3   Each Partner shall at all times duly and punctually pay and discharge his or
           her separate and private debts and engagements whether present or future
           and keep the property of the Partnership and the other Partners and their
           personal representatives estates and effects indemnified therefrom and from
           all actions proceedings costs claims and demands in respect thereof

---

[6]   'Resolve' and 'Resolution' are defined terms. See definitions in Schedule I at p 81 and Table M at
      p 84.
[7]   Delete if there will never be less than three partners.
[8]   There is no requirement under the Partnership Act 1890 for any partner to devote any specific
      amount of time to the firm's business.

5. **PARTNERSHIP PROPERTY**

5.1 The Partnership shall be carried on at [*address* and at]⁹ such places as the Partners shall Resolve

5.2 The leases of any premises from time to time used for the purpose of the Partnership and property or securities or other assets of whatsoever kind held by the Partnership at the date hereof or hereafter acquired on behalf of the Partnership shall be the property of the Partnership and shall be held by such of the Partners in whose names the same may from time to time be vested in trust for the Partners in the shares in which they are from time to time entitled to share in capital

5.3 The Partners hereby indemnify any Partner or former Partner in whose name any such property or securities or other assets as aforesaid are for the time being vested (or have previously been vested) against all claims for rent property taxes costs of repairs alterations or improvements and insurance relating to any such property and generally in respect of any obligations in respect of any such property securities or other assets¹⁰

6. **HOLIDAYS AND INCAPACITY**

6.1 Each Partner shall be entitled (in addition to statutory holidays) to [4] weeks holiday in each calendar year or to such other periods as the Partners may from time to time Resolve

6.2 Without prejudice to the provisions of Clause T2 any Partner who shall be incapacitated (except by reason of pregnancy)¹¹ from carrying out his or her duties for a total of [125 working days]¹² in any period of [18 months] shall be automatically suspended from acting as a Partner until he or she shall be certified by a doctor as fit to resume full-time work and shall have resumed his or her duties

7. **PARTNER'S INSURANCE**

Unless otherwise Resolved by the Partners every Partner shall make provision for retirement through the medium of retirement annuities or personal pension schemes by applying in each Accounting Period not less than [17.5%] of his or her profit share before taxation for the previous Accounting Period (not exceeding the maximum amount allowed under Sections 619 and 640 of the Income and Corporation Taxes Act 1988 as

---

⁹ Traditional partnership agreements include the address of the firm's premises but this may not be necessary unless there are special circumstances.

¹⁰ Although such an indemnity is implied, an express indemnity is better. As a result of the recession in the early 1990s, a number of ex-partners have found themselves being sued on leases they signed for their firms many years ago, often without any formal documentation still in existence to prove their indemnity rights. Put a copy of your Partnership Agreement with your will!

¹¹ Consideration should be given to specific pregnancy leave. See Precedent 1: Standard Partnership Agreement, Clause 6.3 at p 28.

¹² Quote periods of absence in working days rather than months. This prevents a sick partner from appearing at the office on a stretcher for a day or two, in order to start the 6 months' sick leave again!

amended from time to time) in payment of premiums therefor or contributions thereto[13]

8.   RESTRICTIONS

Subject to the provisions of this Agreement and unless otherwise Resolved no Partner shall:

8.1   engage directly or indirectly in any business other than that of the Firm[14]

8.2   engage or (except for gross misconduct) dismiss any member of the staff of the Firm (other than staff working specifically for that Partner and then only after following due statutory procedures)[15]

8.3   employ any of the money goods or effects of the Firm or pledge the credit thereof except in the ordinary course of business and upon the account or for the benefit of the Firm

8.4   lend money or give credit on behalf of the Firm to or have any dealings with any person firm or company whom the Partners shall have previously Resolved not to treat or deal with

8.5   buy order or contract for any goods articles or property on behalf of the Firm in excess of [£1,000] in any one transaction[16]

8.6   enter into any bond or become bail surety or security with or for any person or do or knowingly cause or suffer to be done anything whereby the Partnership property or any part thereof may be seized attached or taken in execution[17]

---

[13] Many professional firms now insist on partners making adequate provision for their retirement through personal pension plans. Many partners argue that this is not an area in which the other partners should interfere; that provision for retirement should be a matter for the choice of each partner. I disagree. Substantial moral pressure can be placed upon partners when a partner who has not made adequate provision reaches retirement age, to make some special arrangement as the partner cannot afford to retire. In firms where progression to larger equity shares is by negotiation, older partners are not willing to reduce their profit shares, because they need the earnings to provide for pension. Similarly, problems can arise if partners die before retirement or retire due to ill health without having made adequate provision.

For all of these reasons, provisions requiring partners to contribute to pension are essential. Pension provision is a very tax effective form of investment for the self-employed. Premiums (up to the statutory limit) are fully deductible for income tax, and the resultant cash at retirement is tax free as to capital withdrawn and earned income as to pension.

[14] It is assumed that partners will work full-time for the firm. Many partnership problems arise because of involvement of individual partners in outside business enterprises, and these should be discouraged, unless they are for the direct benefit of the firm.

[15] In any but the smallest firms, management authority is delegated to an individual partner or committee, and individual partners should be restrained from treating the firm as their private fief.

[16] See note 15 above.

[17] Another aspect of the unlimited liability of partners is that the firm is at risk of having its assets attacked if a partner does not meet his or her personal obligations. This clause would give grounds for expulsion if the firm's assets were attacked by a partner's creditors. Expulsion would not necessarily be justified if there was no real risk to the firm.

8.7   assign mortgage or charge his or her share in the Partnership or any part of such share[18]

[9.   PREVIOUS AGREEMENTS
           Save in respect of continuing obligations to former Partners the previous Partnership Agreement dated [. . .] [(as varied by Resolution)] shall forthwith cease to have effect]

10.   VARIATION OF AGREEMENT
10.1   Subject as herein otherwise expressly provided the terms and provisions of this Agreement relating to financial matters (including by way of example but not of limitation shares of profit contributions to capital and repayment of capital) or voting rights may be varied by Resolution of the Partners

10.2   Subject as herein otherwise expressly provided any other terms and conditions of this Agreement may also be varied by Resolution of the Partners

10.3   No variation pursuant to this Clause shall take effect so as to prejudice the rights of any former Partner

10.4   Upon any variation of this Agreement amendments shall be made to the relevant page or pages or a new page or new pages shall be inserted in the Agreement and in either case shall be signed by [any 2 Partners] A copy of the page or pages as amended or substituted shall be supplied to each Partner as soon as practical after signature[19]

11.   GENERAL
11.1   Save as herein otherwise provided all disputes and questions whatsoever which shall either during the Partnership or afterwards arise between the Partners or their respective personal representatives shall be referred to a single arbitrator who shall be appointed by the Partners involved in the dispute if they can agree upon one or (failing agreement) by the [President for the time being of the [*body*]] on the application of any Partner or personal representative and in either case in accordance with and subject to the provisions of the Arbitration Acts 1950 to 1979[20]

11.2   Any notice authorised or required to be given or served by this Agreement shall be deemed to be duly served if the same shall be delivered personally

---

[18]   Assigning a share does not make the assignee a partner. It merely gives him or her a right to receive a share of the profits, not to act as partner. See the Partnership Act 1890, s 31 (see Appendix).

[19]   This clause gives effect to the loose-leaf principles of this form of Agreement. This Agreement will be executed with one master copy and copies held by partners in a ring binder which can be updated as appropriate. I recommend that each page of the original document should be initialled by one partner for identification purposes. It is recommended that original pages which are amended are retained with the master copy. See 'About the Precedents' in the Introduction and the Partnership Act 1890, s 19.

[20]   Partnership disputes before the courts should be avoided. Arbitration is a most suitable procedure for partners. Some firms name the arbitrator in their Agreement, often their solicitor.

to the person to whom it is intended to be given or shall be sent by post
in a pre-paid letter sent by recorded delivery or by registered post and
addressed to him or her at his or her last known place of abode in England
or (if it is reasonable to expect that he or she will receive it within 72
hours) left for him or her in the room of the Partnership premises in which
he or she habitually worked as a Partner and where so sent or left shall be
deemed to be served on the first working day of the Firm which shall
follow the day on which such letter would in the ordinary course of post
have been delivered or the day on which the same shall have been left

11.3   A notice to the Partners shall be properly served if delivered to or served
          upon any [3] Partners in accordance with this Clause

SCHEDULE D

Dissolution Provisions

D1   DISSOLUTION

The Partnership may be dissolved by a Resolution[21] of the Partners and shall be dissolved in accordance with Clause 3.3

D2   DISTRIBUTION OF NET ASSETS

Upon the dissolution of the Partnership the assets and credits shall be sold or realised as soon as practicable and the proceeds applied

D2.1   first in paying and discharging the debts and liabilities of the Partnership and the expenses of and incidental to the winding up of the affairs of the Partnership any deficiency being contributed rateably by the Partners in the proportions in which they shared profits[22] immediately prior to dissolution

D2.2   second in paying to those Partners who have made Tax Reserves the amount of such Tax Reserves [together with interest accrued on such Tax Reserves] in accordance with Clause F6.1 up to the date of dissolution and as between such Partners rateably according to the total of such Tax Reserves

D2.3   third in repaying to the Partners rateably their Capital Accounts but so that no payment shall be made to a Partner whose Capital Account is less than his or her due proportion until repayments of Capital Account to other Partners have reduced their Capital Accounts to a similar proportional level

D2.4   fourth in paying any surplus rateably to the Partners in the proportions in which they shared profits[23] immediately prior to dissolution

D3   EXECUTION OF DOCUMENTS

The Partners respectively shall execute do or concur in all necessary or proper instruments acts matters and things for effecting or facilitating the getting in sale and realisation of the assets and credits of the Partnership and the due application and division of the proceeds thereof and for their mutual release or indemnity or otherwise

---

[21] 'Resolve' and 'Resolution' are defined terms. See definitions in Schedule I at p 81 and Table M at p 84.

[22] Note that profit shares determine the contribution to any deficiency and the distribution of any surplus on dissolution. Consideration should be given to amending these clauses if capital shares differ from profit shares.

[23] See note 22 above.

D4　　　RESTRICTION ON USE OF FIRM'S NAME
　　　　No Partner shall be entitled to practise after the date of dissolution under
　　　　the Firm Name unless and to the extent that he or she shall have been
　　　　authorised to do so by all of the other Partners

SCHEDULE F

Financial Provisions

F1   CAPITAL[24]

F1.1   The capital of the Partnership shall be the amount[25] contributed as set out in Table F or such other amount as the Partners shall Resolve[26]

F1.2   Any further capital required by the Partnership shall be contributed by the Partners in the proportions in which they are entitled to share in profits

F2   PROFIT SHARES[27]

F2.1   The profits of the Partnership [after payment of interest pursuant to Clause F6.1] shall be divided between the Partners in the shares set out against the name of each Partner in Table F subject to the provisions of this Clause

F2.2   In respect of a Partner who is incapacitated from carrying out his or her duties for the period set out in Clause 6.2 the profit share due to such Partner shall cease to accrue to such Partner from the end of such period of incapacity until he or she shall have resumed his or her duties in accordance with Clause 6.2

F3   DRAWINGS

Each Partner shall be at liberty to draw out for his or her separate use on account of his or her accruing profit share for the then current Accounting Period the monthly amount set against his or her name in Table F[28]

F4   ANNUAL ACCOUNTS

F4.1   The Annual Accounts shall be prepared as soon as practical after each Accounting Date by reference to generally accepted accounting principles

---

[24] Partners are not entitled to interest on capital before signature of the Firm's Accounts (Partnership Act 1890, s 24(4)). Inequality of contribution can be dealt with by inserting a provision for payment of interest on capital.

[25] See note 31 below as to reserves.

[26] 'Resolve' and 'Resolution' are defined terms. See definitions in Schedule I at p 81 and Table M at p 84.

[27] See Precedent 4: Trading Firm Partnership Agreement, Clause F2 at p 122 for an example of Partners' 'salaries' plus profit share.

[28] It is a good discipline to establish fixed drawing limits for partners as a protection against overdrawing. In the absence of agreement, partners are not allowed drawings until after the signature of the partnership accounts.

F4.2   The Annual Accounts shall be signed by all the Partners and when so
            signed shall be binding on all the Partners except that if any manifest error
            therein be detected within 6 months after such signature such error shall
            be rectified immediately

F4.3   The Annual Accounts shall be prepared on the basis that (unless otherwise
            Resolved)[29]:

            F4.3.1   the goodwill of the Partnership shall be treated as having no value
                      and the value thereof (if any) shall not feature therein
            F4.3.2   the Annual Accounts for each Accounting Period shall be
                      prepared on a consistent basis with the previous Annual Accounts
                      (if any)

F5   DISTRIBUTION OF PROFITS[30]
F5.1   The profits of the Partnership in each Accounting Period after taking into
            account drawings and such reserves as shall be Resolved upon by the
            Partners [on the advice of the Partnership Accountants][31] (including the
            reserves referred to in Clause F6.1) shall be divided between the Partners
            immediately after they have signed the Annual Accounts in respect of that
            Accounting Period[32]

F5.2   If it shall appear at any time that any Partner has drawn out more than the
            amount of drawings authorised pursuant to Clause F3 or more than his or
            her profit share in respect of any Accounting Period that Partner shall
            forthwith repay the deficiency to the Partnership and until such repayment
            the amount of such deficiency shall be a first charge on and be set off
            against future drawings [and shall bear interest at [2 per cent per annum
            over the base rate for the time being of the Firm's bankers calculated with
            3-monthly rests][33] from the last day of that Accounting Period until
            repayment][34]

---

[29] See note 55 below.

[30] Partners in smaller firms frequently leave excess capital (or undrawn profits) in the firm. In such
      event, consideration should be given to introducing the concept of advances as in Schedule F in
      Precedent 1: Standard Partnership Agreement, see p 38.

[31] Clearly, advice will be taken from the partnership accountants in relation to tax reserves, but this
      clause is a reminder that other reserves may cause some contention between partners – eg a sinking
      fund for building refurbishment or purchase. This issue should be considered in connection with
      Clause F1.1, as a permanent requirement for reserve should be dealt with as an increase in capital.
      This clause *obliges* the partners to obtain advice from the accountants, which can take the heat out
      of the argument.

[32] A reminder that partners are entitled to draw their surplus profits after signature of the accounts. If
      the partnership cannot afford a run on its bank account, then the partners should decide to reserve
      or increase capital.

[33] The rate at which the firm borrows money from its bank would seem appropriate.

[34] As partners are not normally entitled to interest on capital (see note 24 above), it may be appropriate
      to charge interest to overdrawn partners.

F6   **TAXATION**[35]

F6.1   In respect of each Accounting Period [to which Section 215 of the Finance Act 1994 applies] the Partners shall Resolve upon the amount of income tax which they estimate [on the advice of the Partnership Accountants][36] to be payable by each Partner in respect of such period[37] and which they shall transfer to Tax Reserve in respect of each Partner. Each such reserve shall be retained until an assessment to income tax is made upon the relevant Partner and the amount of the assessment (or so much thereof as is represented by the reserve) shall be paid to H.M. Collector of Taxes on the date when the assessment is due for payment. Any surplus of the reserve made in respect of that assessment shall thereupon be repaid to the relevant Partner and any deficiency shall be provided by the relevant Partner out of his or her own resources. Such reserves shall carry interest at [the base rate for the time being of the Firm's bankers calculated with 3-monthly rests][38] from the date of the Resolution until payment (or at such other rate and on such other basis as may be determined by a Resolution of the Partners)

F6.2   Upon or after any Partner ceasing to be a Partner [(unless by reason thereof the Partnership shall be dissolved)][39] and upon or after the admission of any new Partner all Partners (including a new Partner and any former Partner and the personal representatives of any deceased Partner) shall if so Resolved by the Partners join in giving to H.M. Inspector of Taxes or any other requisite authority in such form as may be required any notice and join in making any election or the withdrawal or amendment thereof relating to any fiscal matter in connection with the affairs of the Partnership and for this purpose shall sign any such document and do any such act and provide any such information as shall be necessary to give effect to such Resolution. The Partners may Resolve to nominate a

---

[35] This clause is drafted to deal with both the new tax rules for partnerships under the Finance Act 1994, s 215 (replacing the Income and Corporation Taxes Act 1988, s 111, and also firms which still have the opportunity to make a continuation election under the old Income and Corporation Taxes Act 1988, s 113. (These are firms which commenced trade before 6 April 1994 and which have not decided to adopt an actual basis of taxation.) For firms which are on the new basis at the time of signature of the Agreement and which have no 'open' years on the old basis, the words in brackets in the first two lines of Clause F6.1 and Clauses F6.2 to F6.4 can be deleted. See heading 'Taxation' in 'About the Law' in the Introduction.

[36] See note 31 above.

[37] Even though the partners have no joint liability for income tax under the new rules, it is considered desirable not to permit partners to draw against profits on the basis that they will settle their own tax when the bill arrives. For some partners, the temptation to spend the apparent extra income may be difficult to resist. Most existing firms already reserve for tax and most existing partners will be prepared to accept a continuation of present practice. In most firms the partnership accountants will continue to prepare the tax computations.

[38] A rate should be selected which encourages partners to leave capital with the firm and which has some advantage to the firm as well. Base rate seems appropriate.

[39] Delete if there will never be less than three partners.

Partner to sign such document on behalf of some or all of the Partners[40]

F6.3   The Partners shall indemnify any former Partner and his or her estate and effects from and against any taxation of whatsoever nature suffered by him or her or his or her estate as a result of ceasing to be a Partner in excess of what would have been suffered by such former Partner or his or her estate and effects had such notice or election or withdrawal or amendment thereof (as the case may be) not been given

[F6.4   The Partners (other than the new Partner to whom the indemnity is given) shall indemnify any new Partner from and against any taxation of whatsoever nature suffered in excess of what would have been suffered by such new Partner as a result of his or her admission as a Partner had such notice or election or withdrawal or amendment thereof (as the case may be) not been given][41]

F7   BOOKS OF ACCOUNT
All proper and usual books of account and entries therein shall be kept (in either paper or electronic form) by the Partners and each Partner shall ensure that full and proper entries are duly and punctually made of all business transacted by him or her or at his or her direction on account of the Firm

F8   BANKING
F8.1   The Firm shall maintain bank accounts with such bankers as the Partners shall from time to time Resolve

F8.2   All Partnership monies (not required for current expenses) and securities for monies shall as and when received be paid into or deposited with the Firm's bankers for the credit of the Firm's accounts. All cheques on such accounts shall be drawn by any [1] Partner in respect of amounts under [£1,000] for any one payee and by any [2] Partners in respect of amounts of [£1,000] or over unless otherwise Resolved by the Partners

---

[40]   Under the 'old' regime, unless an election is made under the Income and Corporation Taxes Act 1988, s 113 the firm has a 'cessation' for tax purposes on a partner leaving or joining the firm. A cessation is the 'default' position and so the indemnity is given if there is a continuation. However, if profits are reducing a partner who leaves may have an additional tax liability if no election to continue is made.

[41]   Many firms do not consider it appropriate to give this indemnity to an incoming partner.

TABLE F[42]

Capital Contributions Profit Shares and Drawings

Capital contributions[43] profit shares[44] and drawings[45] with effect from the [. . .] day of [. . .] 199[. . .] shall be as follows:

Partner	Capital	Profit share	Monthly drawings
[name (1)]	£	[. . .]%	£
[name (2)]	£	[. . .]%	£
[name (3)]	£	[. . .]%	£
[name (4)]	£	[. . .]%	£
Total	£	100%	£

---

[42]   Tables are placed on separate pages for ease of replacement. See Clause 10.4 and note 19 at p 71.
[43]   See Clause F1 at p 75.
[44]   See Clause F2 at p 75.
[45]   See Clause F3 at p 75.

SCHEDULE I

Interpretation and Definitions

I1   DEFINITIONS
            In this Agreement the following expressions shall where the context so
            admits have the following meanings:

'Accounting Date'	the date up to which the Annual Accounts are drawn and until otherwise Resolved[46] the [. . .] day of [. . .] in each year
'Annual Accounts'	the accounts drawn in accordance with Schedule F
'Accounting Period'	the period from one Accounting Date to the next Accounting Date
'Capital Account'	in relation to any Partner his or her share of the capital of the Partnership in accordance with Clause F1
'Eligible Votes'[47]	the votes of all Partners whether or not attending a meeting except a Partner disqualified from voting pursuant to Clause M3
'Firm'	the business carried on by the Partners in partnership under the Firm Name pursuant to this Agreement
'Firm Name'	[X Y and Z] or any colourable imitation thereof or any combination of names which include any or all of [X Y or Z] or any colourable imitation of any such respective names
'Partners'	the persons whose names are set out in Schedule P and where the context so admits such of them as shall continue to

---

[46] 'Resolve' and 'Resolution' are defined terms. See definitions in this Schedule and Table M at
      p 84.
[47] This definition needs careful consideration. Is voting by:
      1   all partners?; or
      2   all partners who attend a meeting?; and
      3   votes by percentage of capital or votes allocated per partner? (For an example of allocation see
          Precedent 4: Trading Firm Partnership Agreement, Clause M2.1 at p 131 and Schedule P at
          p 135.)

	be Partners in the Partnership and any other future Partners for the time being but not any salaried partners
'the Partnership'	the partnership [presently subsisting *or* created hereby] between the Partners including any partnership which is a successor to that partnership under whatever name
'Partnership Accountants'	Messrs [...] or such other chartered accountants as the Partners shall Resolve
'Resolve' and 'Resolution'	to determine in accordance with Schedule M
'Retirement Capital'	a sum equal to the amount of capital standing to the credit of a Partner in his or her Capital Account on his or her Termination Date after adding his or her profit share (after actual drawings) from the previous Accounting Date until his or her Termination Date and after deducting therefrom

1. (if the Partner shall have been expelled from the Partnership pursuant to Clause T3) such sum as the remaining Partners shall Resolve to be necessary or sufficient to discharge all or any liability of the Partnership directly or indirectly attributable to the conduct of the Partner

[2. such sum as [in the opinion of the Partnership Accountants] may be required to satisfy his or her share of any income tax assessment which may be made upon the Partnership for any year of assessment ended prior to his or her Termination Date; and

3. the appropriate proportion of his or her share of any income tax assessment for the year of assessment in which he or she ceases to be a Partner][48]

---

[48] For firms which are on the new tax rules for partnerships under the Finance Act 1994, s 215 (replacing the Income and Corporation Taxes Act 1988, s 111) (see Appendix) at the time of signature of the Agreement and which have no 'open' years on the old basis, the words in brackets can be deleted. See note 35 above.

'Retirement Interest'	interest at [. . . per cent per annum above the base rate of [. . .] Bank plc from time to time] computed with [6-monthly] rests[49]
['Succession Notice'	a notice in writing pursuant to Clause T4]
'Table F'	the table at the end of Schedule F
'Table M'	the table at the end of Schedule M
'Tax Reserve'	the amount standing to the credit of a Partner in the books of the Partnership for that Partner's reserve for taxation pursuant to Clause F6.1
'Termination Date'	the date on which a Partner ceases to be a Partner whether pursuant to this Agreement or by death

I2.   INTERPRETATION

I2.1   Headings to Clauses and Schedules are for ease of reference only and shall be of no effect in construing the provisions of this Agreement

I2.2   Where the context so admits:

        I2.2.1   words importing the singular number shall include the plural and words importing the plural number shall include the singular

        I2.2.2   references to statutes or to sections of statutes shall include any statutory modifications or re-enactments thereof for the time being in force

---

[49]   The interest rate could be the same as the rate at which the firm borrows funds from its bankers. There is no reason for the firm to profit from the capital of a retired partner, although its retention will help cash flow.

SCHEDULE M

Meetings and Voting

M1 **PARTNERS MEETINGS**
The Partners shall meet for the purpose of dealing with Partnership matters at times and dates of which at least [one week's][50] notice shall be given by any Partner to all Partners (except in case of emergency)

M2 **VOTING RESTRICTIONS**
A Partner shall not be entitled to vote on a Resolution[51]:

M2.1 To cause his or her retirement by reason of incapacity pursuant to Clause T2

M2.2 To expel him or her pursuant to Clause T3

M3 **VOTING PERCENTAGES**
M3.1 For a Resolution to be passed arising under the Clause set out in column 1 of Table M a brief description of which (for convenience and not by way of construction) is set out in column 2 of Table M the percentage of Eligible Votes[52] set out in column 3 of Table M must be in favour of the Resolution

M3.2 All decisions of the Partners which do not arise under any Clause shall be made by Resolution

---

[50] The period and formalities of notice will vary according to the size of the firm and the location of its offices.

[51] 'Resolve' and 'Resolution' are defined terms. See definitions in Schedule I at p 81 and Table M at p 84.

[52] Careful consideration needs to be given to this definition.

TABLE M[53]

Voting Percentages

Clause	Brief description	Percentage of Eligible Votes[54]
2.2	Change Firm Name	[51]
3.1	Admit new Partner	[100]
5.1	Change Partnership premises	[75]
6.1	Change holiday entitlement	[51]
7	Change pension provision	[75]
8	Waive restrictions	[75]
8.4	Not to act for client	[51]
10.1	Vary Agreement – financial/voting	[100]
10.2	Vary Agreement – other	[51]
D1	Dissolve Partnership	[100]
F1.1	Fix Partnership capital	[100]
F4.3	Change accounting basis[55]	[100]
F5.1	Agree reserves	[75]
F6.1	Estimate Tax Reserves	[75]
F6.1	Vary interest on Tax Reserves	[75]
F6.2	Sign tax election	[75]
F8.1	Change bank	[51]
F8.2	Change bank mandate	[51]

[53] Tables are placed on separate pages for ease of replacement. See Clause 10.4 and note 19 at p 71.
[54] All of the percentages in this Table are merely suggestions.
[55] This resolution may well have the effect of penalising a partner on changes in shares, or retirement. For example, a decision in a professional firm to change the basis on which work in progress is valued (or in a trading company to change the basis of stock valuation), or to change the basis of depreciation, will have the effect of altering the profits which arise in that accounting period.

Clause		Brief description	Percentage of Eligible Votes
I1		Change Accounting Date[56]	[100]
I1		Change Partnership Accountants	[51]
M3.2		Resolution not varying the Agreement	[51]
T2	★	Retire Partner for incapacity	[100]
T3	★	Expel Partner	[100]

★Clause M2 restricts entitlement to vote on these Resolutions

---

[56] 100% is suggested for changing the accounting date as it may have implications for profit shares (if shares change at the end of an accounting period), and also for retirement date.

SCHEDULE P

The Partners

Name and address	Identifying initials	Date joined	Date ceased

SCHEDULE T

Termination and Repayment Provisions

Part 1
Termination[57]

T1   **RETIREMENT BY AGE OR NOTICE**[57]

Each Partner shall retire on the Accounting Date following his or her [65th] birthday and may (if he or she shall give to the other Partners not less than [6] months' notice in writing of his or her intention to do so) retire from the Partnership on any Accounting Date [and if only one Partner shall remain following such retirement, the Partnership shall be dissolved in accordance with Schedule D unless a Succession Notice shall be given in accordance with Clause T4][58]

T2   **RETIREMENT DUE TO INCAPACITY**

If a Partner has been or in the view of competent medical opinion is likely to be incapacitated from carrying out his or her duties as a Partner for the total period set out in Clause 6.2 (and without prejudice to the provisions of Clause 6.2) then the Partners may Resolve[59] that such Partner shall retire from the Partnership on the date specified in the Resolution by reason of incapacity in which event he or she shall cease to be a Partner on such date [and if only one Partner shall remain following such retirement, the Partnership shall be dissolved in accordance with Schedule D unless a Succession Notice shall be given in accordance with Clause T4]

T3   **EXPULSION**

T3.1   If any Partner shall:

         T3.1.1   charge assign or transfer his or her share in the Partnership or any part thereof or suffer the same to be charged for his or her separate debt under the Partnership Act 1890

         T3.1.2   become bankrupt or insolvent or compound or make any arrangement with or for the benefit of his or her creditors or

---

[57]   Consider whether a provision for compulsory retirement is appropriate to the firm. See Precedent 1: Standard Partnership Agreement, Clause T8 at p 60.

[58]   This precedent contains an option for the remaining partner of two to acquire the business. See notes 61, 62 below.

[59]   'Resolve' and 'Resolution' are defined terms. See definitions in Schedule I at p 81 and Table M at p 84.

apply for an interim order pursuant to Section 253 of the Insolvency Act 1986 or have a petition for a bankruptcy order against him or her presented to the Court

T3.1.3   act in any manner inconsistent with the good faith observable between Partners

T3.1.4   be guilty of any conduct which would be a ground for dissolution of the Partnership by the Court

T3.1.5   absent himself or herself from the Partnership without proper cause for more than [4] weeks (consecutive or otherwise) in any period of 12 months[60]

T3.1.6   be convicted of any offence involving fraud or dishonesty or be sentenced to a term of imprisonment whether or not suspended

T3.1.7   be suspended or expelled by the [*body*]

T3.1.8   be guilty of any flagrantly immoral behaviour or of any flagrant grave deliberate or persistent breach or breaches of the ethics or etiquette of the [. . .] profession or of any other conduct calculated or tending to injure the reputation of the Firm or likely to have a serious or adverse effect upon the Firm's business

T3.1.9   commit any substantial breach of this Agreement

then and in any such case the Partners may Resolve to determine the Partnership so far as it concerns such Partner on the date specified in the Resolution in which event he or she shall cease to be a Partner on such date [and if only one Partner shall remain following such expulsion, the Partnership shall be dissolved in accordance with Schedule D unless a Succession Notice shall be given in accordance with Clause T4]

T3.2   If any question shall arise concerning the existence of the grounds for expulsion or exercise of the power to expel conferred by Clause T3.1 such question shall be referred to arbitration under the provisions of Clause 11.1

[T4   SUCCESSION NOTICE
T4.1   If, following termination, there shall be only one Partner, that Partner may

T4.1.1   within [one month] of receiving notice pursuant to clause T1;[61] or

T4.1.2   within [6] months prior to the Accounting Date following the other Partner's 65th birthday; or

---

[60] Even 4 weeks may be too long for unexplained absences!

[61] This can be a two-edged sword. On the one hand, it is not fair that a partner who wishes to continue should be forced to have a dissolution just because the other partner wishes to retire (or at least to have the threat of a dissolution used in negotiations). On the other hand, if two partners are in dispute, why should the one who resigns, possibly because he or she cannot stand the aggravation, be penalised by losing the business. This is an issue which should be brought to clients' attention so that they can decide!

T4.1.3   at the time of giving notice pursuant to clauses T2[62] or T3 or before the expiry thereof; or

T4.1.4   within [one month] of the date of death of the other Partner[63]

give a Succession Notice to the other Partner (or his or her personal representatives as the case may be)

T4.2   If a Succession Notice shall be served the Partner serving the Succession Notice shall acquire the share of the other Partner in accordance with Part 2 of this Schedule and Schedule D shall not apply]

Part 2
Repayment and consequent provisions
[If, following Termination, there shall be only one Partner, this Part of this Schedule shall only have effect if a Succession Notice shall have been served]

T5   PAYMENT
Upon any Partner ceasing to be a Partner

[T5.1   any Tax Reserve held for him or her together with all accrued interest at his or her Termination Date shall be repaid to him or her or his or her personal representatives within [3] months from his or her Termination Date]

T5.2   the Retirement Capital of such Partner shall be repaid to him or her (or his or her personal representatives) by [6] equal [6-monthly] instalments the first of such instalments to be paid to him or her (or his or her personal representatives) [6] months after his or her Termination Date

T5.3   Retirement Interest calculated from the Termination Date shall be paid with each payment of his or her Retirement Capital [and his or her Tax Reserve]

T6   RETENTIONS
Sums retained from Retirement Capital for income tax which are not required to satisfy a Partner's share of any income tax assessments shall be credited to the Partner's Retirement Capital (or paid to him or her if his or her Retirement Capital has been repaid) as soon as the relevant income tax assessment has been agreed with the Inland Revenue and any deficiency in any sum so retained shall be reimbursed by the Partner on demand

---

[62]   It is difficult to decide what is fair. Obviously, if a partner has been sick for some time, it would be unfair for the continuing partner to be forced to have a dissolution of the firm. But is it fair to the sick partner that the other partner should be able to force a dissolution, with the attendant advantage in acquiring the business? Perhaps this option for a succession notice should be to allow *either* partner to require the healthy partner to continue.

[63]   See note 62 above. Perhaps this should also be a two-way notice provision.

T7   GENERAL PROVISIONS

T7.1   Upon a Partner ceasing to be a Partner his or her profit share shown in
            Table F shall be cancelled

T7.2   The remaining Partners shall succeed to all the interest of the former
            Partner in the Partnership (subject to his or her rights herein contained) [in
            the shares which as between themselves they share profits *or* equally][64] and
            shall undertake all the debts liabilities and obligations of the former Partner
            and will indemnify and keep the former Partner indemnified against all
            such debts liabilities and obligations other than such as are hereby deemed
            to be for his or her separate account or are directly or indirectly
            attributable to any act or omission of the former Partner but without
            prejudice to any subsisting liability of the former Partner for breach of this
            Agreement[65]

T7.3   If and so far as it shall be necessary to apportion profits and losses for any
            period the apportionment shall be on a time basis by reference to the then
            current Accounting Period

T7.4   A former Partner shall have no rights whatsoever against any remaining
            Partner save as herein expressly provided

T8   RESTRICTIONS[66]
            A former Partner shall not:

T8.1   at any time solicit whether by himself or herself or as a partner or
            employee of any other person firm or company directly or indirectly any
            person firm or company who shall have been a client of the Firm [other
            than a client personally introduced by him or her to the Firm[67] and other
            than his or her relatives or a company wholly owned or controlled by him
            or her or his or her relatives] at any time during a period of 3 years
            immediately preceding the date when he or she ceased to be a Partner

---

[64] Careful consideration needs to be given to this issue. Allocating a share equally between the
      remaining partners can help in a move towards equality of shares.

[65] This clause can give rise to many difficulties.
          First, it must be made clear that a partner will not be indemnified against his or her own default.
      So a partner who is expelled for cause remains liable to indemnify his former partners against loss
      arising from that default.
          Second, a partner who is negligent remains liable to indemnify for his or her own negligence. This
      is not an issue if the firm has sufficient negligence insurance to cover a claim, as the insurance extends
      to all partners, including one who is negligent. Moreover, in most cases of negligence, the claim
      rarely arises exclusively from one person's mistake, making claims difficult to pursue inside a firm.
          Third is the liability of all partners for negligence claims in excess of the firm's insurance cover. My
      view is that if such a claim has been intimated at the termination date, a reserve should be included
      in the retirement accounts but, if not, the former partner should get a full indemnity against future
      claims, whenever the negligent act happened.

[66] These restrictions are by way of guidance only. Careful consideration must be given in each case
      having regard to the size of the firm, its business, its location and the other factors taken into account
      when considering the enforceability of restrictive covenants.

[67] Disputes can arise over introductions of business unless the firm has a well-settled procedure for
      identifying introducers.

T8.2 during a period of 3 years from the date of ceasing to be a Partner carry on or be concerned or engaged or interested whether directly or indirectly and whether by himself or herself or as a partner or employee of any other person firm or company in the [practice or profession of *or* business of . . .] within a radius of [one mile] from any address at which at the date of his or her ceasing to be a partner the Firm shall be carrying on the Partnership business

T8.3 at any time after ceasing to be a Partner and in any place carry on business under any style or name which shall include or refer to the Firm Name

T8.4 at any time suggest or cause to be suggested to any member of the Firm's staff that he or she might leave the employment of the Firm to work for the former Partner or for any company or firm with which the former Partner is or intends to be connected

T9 **SEVERANCE OF RESTRICTIONS**
It is hereby declared that the provisions of each of Clauses T8.1 to T8.4 respectively are intended to be read and construed independently of each other so that none of such separate provisions shall be dependent on any one or more of any of the other such provisions

SCHEDULE X

Execution

This Deed is intended to be delivered by each Partner on the date of delivery opposite that Partner's name

Name of Partner	Signature as a Deed	Date of Delivery	Signature of Witness
[name (1)]	....		....
[name (2)]	....		....
[name (3)]	....		....
[name (4)]	....		....

PRECEDENT 3: TWO-PARTNER FIRM PARTNERSHIP AGREEMENT FOR A PROFESSIONAL FIRM WITH OPTION FOR ONE PARTNER TO CONTINUE

CONTENTS

PRECEDENT 3: TWO–PARTNER FIRM PARTNERSHIP AGREEMENT[1] FOR A PROFESSIONAL FIRM WITH OPTION FOR ONE PARTNER TO CONTINUE

THIS PARTNERSHIP AGREEMENT[2] dated the [. . .] day of [. . .] 199[. . .][3] BETWEEN

(1) *name (1)*
(2) *name (2)*

executed as a Deed[4] constitutes the terms on which the parties have agreed to carry on business in partnership as [*trade or profession*]

1.   THE SCHEDULES
        This Agreement includes the following Schedules and Tables:

        Schedule F[5]   which contains **F**inancial provisions
        Table F   which contains details of capital profit shares and draw-
                         ings
        Schedule I   which contains **I**nterpretation of this Agreement and
                         definitions used in this Agreement
        Schedule T   which contains **T**ermination and dissolution provisions
        Schedule X   which contains e**X**ecution of this Agreement by the
                         Partners

2.   DURATION – FIRM NAME
2.1   The Partnership shall continue until terminated in accordance with the
        provisions of this Agreement

2.2   The Partnership shall be carried on under the Firm Name or such other
        name or names as the Partners shall agree[6]

---

[1] This precedent is only suitable for two partners. If the firm is likely to grow, Precedent 2: Small Firm Partnership Agreement should be used. This precedent is not suitable for a partnership with a sleeping partner (eg a firm with an investor and an active working partner). Suitable clauses can be found in Precedent 4: Trading Firm Agreement, particularly in Schedule M, see p 131.

[2] See 'About the Precedents' in the Introduction which describes the numbering system used in the precedents. First-time users of this precedent should read Schedule I (Interpretation) first.

[3] See 'About the Precedents' in the Introduction and the Partnership Act 1890, s 19 (see Appendix) as to variation of partnership deeds.

[4] The Agreement is executed as a deed (Schedule X) to give effect to the following clauses:
     3.3   indemnity as to private debts;
     4.2   trust of property (desirable not essential);
     4.3   property indemnity.

[5] See note 1 above.

[6] 'Agree'. As there are only two partners in this precedent, decisions must, of necessity, be unanimous.

3.   GENERAL DUTIES OF THE PARTNERS

3.1   Each Partner shall be just and faithful to the other Partner in all transactions dealings and matters relating to or affecting the Partnership and shall in all circumstances give a true and proper account thereof when reasonably required so to do by the other Partner

3.2   Each Partner shall devote the whole of his or her time and attention to the business of the Firm and diligently and faithfully employ himself or herself therein and use his or her best endeavours to carry on the same for the utmost benefit of the Partnership[7]

3.3   Each Partner shall at all times duly and punctually pay and discharge his or her separate and private debts and engagements whether present or future and keep the property of the Partnership and the other Partner and his or her personal representatives estates and effects indemnified therefrom and from all actions proceedings costs claims and demands in respect thereof

4.   PARTNERSHIP PROPERTY

4.1   The Partnership shall be carried on at [address and at] such places as the Partners shall agree

4.2   The leases of any premises from time to time used for the purpose of the Partnership and property or securities or other assets of whatsoever kind held by the Partnership at the date hereof or hereafter acquired on behalf of the Partnership shall be the property of the Partnership and shall be held by such of the Partners in whose names the same may from time to time be vested in trust for the Partners in the shares in which they are from time to time entitled to share in capital

4.3   The Partners hereby indemnify any Partner or former Partner in whose name any such property or securities or other assets as aforesaid are for the time being vested (or have previously been vested) against all claims for rent property taxes costs of repairs alterations or improvements and insurance relating to any such property and generally in respect of any obligations in respect of any such property securities or other assets[8]

5.   HOLIDAYS AND INCAPACITY

5.1   Each Partner shall be entitled (in addition to statutory holidays) to [4] weeks holiday in each calendar year or to such other periods as the Partners may from time to time agree

5.2   Without prejudice to the provisions of Clause T4 any Partner who shall be

---

[7] There is no requirement under the Partnership Act 1890 for any partner to devote any specific amount of time to the firm's business.

[8] Although such an indemnity is implied, an express indemnity is better. As a result of the recession in the early 1990s, a number of ex-partners have found themselves being sued on leases they signed for their firms many years ago, often without any formal documentation still in existence to prove their indemnity rights. Put a copy of your Partnership Agreement with your will!

incapacitated (except by reason of pregnancy)[9] from carrying out his or her duties for a total of [125 working days][10] in any period of [18 months] shall be automatically suspended from acting as a Partner until he or she shall be certified by a doctor as fit to resume full-time work and shall have resumed his or her duties

6. PARTNER'S INSURANCE
Unless otherwise agreed by the Partners each Partner shall make provision for retirement through the medium of retirement annuities or personal pension schemes by applying in each Accounting Period not less than [17.5%] of his or her profit share before taxation for the previous Accounting Period (not exceeding the maximum amount allowed under Sections 619 and 640 of the Income and Corporation Taxes Act 1988 as amended from time to time) in payment of premiums therefor or contributions thereto[11]

7. RESTRICTIONS
Subject to the provisions of this Agreement and unless otherwise agreed neither Partner shall:

7.1 engage directly or indirectly in any business other than that of the Firm[12]

7.2 employ any of the money goods or effects of the Firm or pledge the credit thereof except in the ordinary course of business and upon the account or for the benefit of the Firm

7.3 lend money or give credit on behalf of the Firm to or have any dealings with any person firm or company whom the other Partner shall have previously requested him or her not to treat or deal with

---

[9] Consideration should be given to specific pregnancy leave. See Precedent 1: Standard Partnership Agreement, Clause 6.3 at p 28.

[10] Quote periods of absence in working days rather than months. This prevents a sick partner from appearing at the office on a stretcher for a day or two, in order to start the 6 months sick leave again! These suggested periods may be too long in the case of a two-person partnership.

[11] Many professional firms now insist on partners making adequate provision for their retirement through personal pension plans. Many partners argue that this is not an area in which the other partners should interfere; that provision for retirement should be a matter for the choice of each partner. I disagree. Substantial moral pressure can be placed upon partners when a partner who has not made adequate provision reaches retirement age, to make some special arrangement as the partner cannot afford to retire. Similarly, problems can arise if partners die before retirement or retire due to ill health without having made adequate provision. For all of these reasons, provisions requiring partners to contribute to a pension are essential. Pension provision is a very tax-effective form of investment for the self-employed. Premiums (up to the statutory limit) are fully deductible for income tax, and the resultant cash at retirement is tax free as to capital withdrawn and earned income as to pension.

[12] It is assumed that partners will work full time for the firm. Many partnership problems arise because of involvement of individual partners in outside business enterprises, and these should be discouraged, unless they are for the direct benefit of the firm.

7.4   buy order or contract for any goods articles or property on behalf of the Firm in excess of [£1,000] in any one transaction[13]

7.5   enter into any bond or become bail surety or security with or for any person or do or knowingly cause or suffer to be done anything whereby the Partnership property or any part thereof may be seized attached or taken in execution[14]

7.6   assign mortgage or charge his or her share in the Partnership or any part of such share[15]

[8.   PREVIOUS AGREEMENTS
        Save in respect of continuing obligations to former Partners the previous Partnership Agreement dated [. . .] shall forthwith cease to have effect]

9.   VARIATION OF AGREEMENT
9.1   No variation of this Agreement shall take effect so as to prejudice the rights of any former Partner

9.2   Upon any variation of this Agreement amendments shall be made to the relevant page or pages or a new page or new pages shall be inserted in the Agreement and in either case shall be signed by both Partners

10.   GENERAL
10.1   Save as herein otherwise provided all disputes and questions whatsoever which shall either during the Partnership or afterwards arise between the Partners or their respective personal representatives shall be referred to a single arbitrator who shall be appointed by the Partners if they can agree upon one or (failing agreement) by the [President for the time being of the [*body*]] on the application of either Partner or his or her personal representative and in either case in accordance with and subject to the provisions of the Arbitration Acts 1950 to 1979[16]

10.2   Any notice authorised or required to be given or served by this Agreement shall be deemed to be duly served if the same shall be delivered personally to the person to whom it is intended to be given or shall be sent by post in a pre-paid letter sent by recorded delivery or by registered post and addressed to him or her at his or her last known place of abode in England and where so sent or left shall be deemed to be served on the first working day of the Firm which shall follow the day on which such letter would in the ordinary course of post have been delivered

---

[13]   Individual partners should be restrained from treating the firm as their private fief.

[14]   Another aspect of the unlimited liability of partners is that the firm is at risk of having its assets attacked if a partner does not meet his or her personal obligations. Breach of this clause could give grounds for dissolution for default (Clause T5.9) if the firm's assets were attacked by a partner's creditors.

[15]   Assigning a share does not make the assignee a partner. It merely gives him or her a right to receive a share of the profits, not to act as partner. See the Partnership Act 1890, s 31 (see Appendix).

[16]   Partnership disputes before the courts should be avoided. Arbitration is a most suitable procedure for partners. Some firms name the arbitrator in their Agreement, often their solicitor.

SCHEDULE F

Financial Provisions

F1 **CAPITAL**

F1.1 The capital of the Partnership shall be the amount[17] contributed as set out in Table F or such other amount as the Partners shall agree[18]

F1.2 Any further capital required by the Partnership shall be contributed by the Partners in the proportions in which they are entitled to share in profits

F2 **PROFIT SHARES**[19]

F2.1 The profits of the Partnership shall be divided between the Partners in the shares set out against the name of each Partner in Table F subject to the provisions of this Clause

F2.2 In respect of a Partner who is incapacitated from carrying out his or her duties for the period set out in Clause 5.2 the profit share due to such Partner shall cease to accrue to such Partner from the end of such period of incapacity until he or she shall have resumed his or her duties in accordance with Clause 5.2

F3 **DRAWINGS**

Each Partner shall be at liberty to draw out for his or her separate use on account of his or her accruing profit share for the then current Accounting Period the monthly amount set against his or her name in Table F[20]

F4 **ANNUAL ACCOUNTS**

F4.1 The Annual Accounts shall be prepared as soon as practical after each Accounting Date by reference to generally accepted accounting principles

F4.2 The Annual Accounts shall be signed by the Partners and when so signed shall be binding on the Partners except that if any manifest error therein be detected within 6 months after such signature such error shall be rectified immediately

---

[17] See note 21 below as to reserves.

[18] Partners are not entitled to interest on capital before signature of the firm's accounts (Partnership Act 1890, s 24(4)). Inequality of contribution can be dealt with by inserting a provision for payment of interest on capital.

[19] See Precedent 4: Trading Firm Partnership Agreement, Clause F2 at p 122 for an example of Partners' 'salaries' plus profit share.

[20] It is a good discipline to establish fixed drawing limits for partners as a protection against overdrawing. In the absence of agreement, partners are not allowed drawings until after the signature of the partnership accounts.

F4.3   The Annual Accounts shall be prepared on the basis that (unless otherwise agreed):

F4.3.1   the goodwill of the Partnership shall be treated as having no value and the value thereof (if any) shall not feature therein

F4.3.2   the Annual Accounts for each Accounting Period shall be prepared on a consistent basis with the previous Annual Accounts (if any)

F5   DISTRIBUTION OF PROFITS[21]

F5.1   The profits of the Partnership in each Accounting Period after taking into account drawings and such reserves[22] as shall be agreed upon by the Partners [on the advice of the Partnership Accountants][23] shall be divided between the Partners immediately after they have signed the Annual Accounts in respect of that Accounting Period[24]

F5.2   If it shall appear at any time that either Partner has drawn out more than the amount of drawings authorised pursuant to Clause F3 or more than his or her profit share in respect of any Accounting Period that Partner shall forthwith repay the deficiency to the Partnership and until such repayment the amount of such deficiency shall be a first charge on and be set off against future drawings [and shall bear interest at [2 per cent per annum over the base rate for the time being of the Firm's bankers calculated with 3-monthly rests][25] from the last day of that Accounting Period until repayment][26]

F6   BOOKS OF ACCOUNT

All proper and usual books of account and entries therein shall be kept (in either paper or electronic form) by the Partners and each Partner shall ensure that full and proper entries are duly and punctually made of all business transacted by him or her or at his or her direction on account of the Firm

---

[21] Partners in smaller firms frequently leave excess capital (or undrawn profits) in the firm. In such event, consideration should be given to introducing the concept of advances as in Schedule F in Precedent 1: Standard Partnership Agreement, see p 38.

[22] Consider whether a tax reserve should be provided. See Precedent 1: Standard Partnership Agreement, Clause F8.1 at p 38 (and related clauses).

[23] Clearly, advice will be taken from the partnership accountants in relation to tax reserves, but this Clause is a reminder that other reserves may cause some contention between partners – eg a sinking fund for building refurbishment or purchase. This issue should be considered in connection with Clause F1.1, as a permanent requirement for reserve should be dealt with as an increase in capital. This clause *obliges* the partners to obtain advice from the accountants, which can take the heat out of the argument.

[24] A reminder that partners are entitled to draw their surplus profits after signature of the accounts. If the partnership cannot afford a run on its bank account, then the partners should decide to reserve or increase capital.

[25] The rate at which the firm borrows money from its bank would seem appropriate.

[26] As partners are not normally entitled to interest on capital (see note 18 above), it may be appropriate to charge interest to overdrawn partners.

F7   BANKING

F7.1   The Firm shall maintain bank accounts with [. . . Bank plc] [. . . branch]
            or such bankers or branch as the Partners shall from time to time agree

F7.2   All Partnership monies (not required for current expenses) and securities
            for monies shall as and when received be paid into or deposited with the
            Firm's bankers for the credit of the Firm's accounts. All cheques on such
            accounts shall be drawn by [one Partner in respect of amounts under
            [£1,000] for any one payee and by] both Partners in respect of amounts of
            [£1,000] or over unless otherwise agreed by the Partners

TABLE F[27]

Capital Contributions Profit Shares and Drawings

Capital contributions[28] profit shares[29] and drawings[30] with effect from the [. . .] day of [. . .] 199[. . .] shall be as follows:

Partner	Capital	Profit share	Monthly drawings
[name (1)]	£	[. . .]%	£
[name (2)]	£	[. . .]%	£
Total	£	100%	£

---

[27]   This Table is placed on a separate page for ease of replacement.
[28]   See Clause F1 at p 99.
[29]   See Clause F2 at p 99.
[30]   See Clause F3 at p 99.

SCHEDULE I

Interpretation and Definitions

I1   DEFINITIONS
       In this Agreement the following expressions shall where the context so
       admits have the following meanings

'Accounting Date'	the date up to which the Annual Accounts are drawn and until otherwise agreed the [. . .] day of [. . .] in each year
'Annual Accounts'	the accounts drawn in accordance with Schedule F
'Accounting Period'	the period from one Accounting Date to the next Accounting Date
'Capital Account'	in relation to any Partner his or her share of the capital of the Partnership in accordance with Clause F1
'Firm'	the business carried on by the Partners in partnership under the Firm Name pursuant to this Agreement
'Firm Name'	[*X Y and Z*] or any colourable imitation thereof or any combination of names which include any or all of [*X Y or Z*] or any colourable imitation of any such respective names
'Partners'	the parties to this agreement and where the context so admits such of them as shall continue to be a Partner in the Partnership and any other future Partners for the time being but not any salaried partners
'the Partnership'	the partnership [presently subsisting *or* created hereby] between the Partners including any partnership which is a successor to that partnership under whatever name
'Partnership Accountants'	Messrs [. . .] or such other chartered accountants as the Partners shall agree
'Retirement Capital'	a sum equal to the amount of capital standing to the credit of a Partner in his or her Capital Account on his or her

	Termination Date [after deducting therefrom

1. such sum as [in the opinion of the Partnership Accountants] may be required to satisfy his or her share of any income tax assessment which may be made upon the Partnership for any year of assessment ended prior to his or her Termination Date; and

2. the appropriate proportion of his or her share of any income tax assessment for the year of assessment in which he or she ceases to be a Partner][31]

'Retirement Interest'	interest at [. . . per cent per annum above the base rate of [. . .] Bank plc from time to time] computed with [6-monthly] rests[32]
['Succession Notice'	a notice in writing pursuant to Clause T6]
'Table F'	the table at the end of Schedule F
'Termination Date'	the date on which a Partner ceases to be a Partner whether pursuant to this Agreement or by death

I2   INTERPRETATION

I2.1   Headings to Clauses and Schedules are for ease of reference only and shall be of no effect in construing the provisions of this Agreement

I2.2   Where the context so admits:

         I2.2.1   words importing the singular number shall include the plural and words importing the plural number shall include the singular

         I2.2.2   references to statutes or to sections of statutes shall include any statutory modifications or re-enactments thereof for the time being in force

---

[31] For firms which are on the new tax rules for partnerships under the Finance Act 1994, s 215 (replacing the Income and Corporation Taxes Act 1988, s 111) (see Appendix) at the time of signature of the Agreement and which have no 'open' years on the old basis, the words in brackets can be deleted. See note 42 below.

[32] The interest rate could be the same as the rate at which the firm borrows funds from its bankers. There is no reason for the firm to profit from the capital of a retired partner, although its retention will help cash flow.

SCHEDULE T

Termination and Dissolution Provisions

Part 1
General

T1   **NOTICE**
Either Partner may by [6] months' notice in writing to the other terminate the Partnership and upon the expiry of such notice the Partnership shall be dissolved[33] [unless a Succession Notice shall be given in accordance with Clause T6][34]

T2   **AGE**
The Partnership shall be dissolved on the elder Partner's [65th] birthday [unless a Succession Notice shall be given in accordance with Clause T6]

T3   **DEATH**
If either Partner shall die the Partnership shall be dissolved [unless a Succession Notice shall be given in accordance with Clause T6]

T4   **INCAPACITY**
If a Partner has been or in the view of competent medical opinion is likely to be incapacitated from carrying out his or her duties as a Partner for the total period set out in Clause 5.2 (and without prejudice to the provisions of Clause 5.2) then the other Partner may serve not less than [one] month's notice in writing on such incapacitated Partner dissolving the Partnership on the date specified in the notice [unless a Succession Notice shall be given in accordance with Clause T6]

T5   **DEFAULT**
If a Partner shall:

T5.1   charge assign or transfer his or her share in the Partnership or any part thereof or suffer the same to be charged for his or her separate debt under the Partnership Act 1890

T5.2   become bankrupt or insolvent or compound or make any arrangement with or for the benefit of his or her creditors or apply for an interim order

---

[33]   Separate clauses are used for resignation, incapacity, and default in order that different periods of notice can apply.

[34]   This precedent contains an option for the remaining partner to acquire the business. See notes 36, 37 below.

pursuant to Section 253 of the Insolvency Act 1986 or have a petition for a bankruptcy order against him or her presented to the Court

T5.3   act in any manner inconsistent with the good faith observable between Partners

T5.4   be guilty of any conduct which would be a ground for dissolution of the Partnership by the Court

T5.5   absent himself or herself from the Partnership without proper cause for more than [4] weeks (consecutive or otherwise) in any period of 12 months[35]

T5.6   be convicted of any offence involving fraud or dishonesty or be sentenced to a term of imprisonment whether or not suspended

T5.7   be suspended or expelled by the [*body*]

T5.8   be guilty of any flagrantly immoral behaviour or of any flagrant grave deliberate or persistent breach or breaches of the ethics or etiquette of the [. . .] profession or of any other conduct calculated or tending to injure the reputation of the Firm or likely to have a serious or adverse effect upon the Firm's business

T5.9   commit any substantial breach of this Agreement

then and in any such case the other Partner may serve notice on the Partner in default dissolving the Partnership on the date specified in the notice [unless a Succession Notice shall be given in accordance with Clause T6]

T6   SUCCESSION NOTICE
T6.1   A Partner may
        T6.1.1 within [one month] of receiving notice pursuant to clause T1;[36] or
        T6.1.2 within [6] months prior to the other Partner's 65th birthday; or
        T6.1.3 at the time of giving notice pursuant to Clauses T4[37] or T5 or before the expiry thereof; or
        T6.1.4 within [one month] of the date of death of the other Partner[38]

---

[35] Even 4 weeks may be too long for unexplained absences!

[36] This can be a two-edged sword. On the one hand, it is not fair that a partner who wishes to continue should be forced to have a dissolution just because the other partner wishes to retire (or at least to have the threat of a dissolution used in negotiations). On the other hand, if two partners are in dispute, why should the one who resigns, possibly because he or she cannot stand the aggravation, be penalised by losing the business. This is an issue which should be brought to clients' attention so that they can decide!

[37] It is difficult to decide what is fair. Obviously, if a partner has been sick for some time, it would be unfair for the continuing partner to be forced to have a dissolution of the firm. But is it fair to the sick partner that the other partner should be able to force a dissolution, with the attendant advantage in acquiring the business? Perhaps this option for a succession notice should be to allow *either* partner to require the healthy partner to continue.

[38] See note 37 above. Perhaps this should also be a two-way notice provision.

give a Succession Notice to the other Partner (or his or her personal representatives as the case may be)

T6.2 If a Succession Notice shall be served the Partner serving the Succession Notice shall acquire the share of the other Partner in accordance with Part 2 of this Schedule and Part 3 of this Schedule shall not apply

T7 WINDING UP
If a Succession Notice shall not be served the Partnership shall be wound up in accordance with Part 3 of this Schedule

T8 EXECUTION OF DOCUMENTS
Each Partner shall execute do or concur in all necessary or proper instruments acts matters and things for effecting or facilitating the winding up of or the succession to the Partnership

Part 2
Succession

T9 GENERAL PROVISIONS
T9.1 The remaining Partner shall succeed to all the interest of the former Partner in the Partnership (subject to his or her rights herein contained) and shall undertake all the debts liabilities and obligations of the former Partner and will indemnify and keep the former Partner indemnified against all such debts liabilities and obligations other than such as are hereby deemed to be for his or her separate account or are directly or indirectly attributable to any act or omission of the former Partner but without prejudice to any subsisting liability of the former Partner for breach of this Agreement[39]

T9.2 The former Partner shall have no rights whatsoever against the remaining Partner save as herein expressly provided

T10 RESTRICTIONS[40]
The former Partner shall not:

T10.1 at any time solicit whether by himself or herself or as a partner or employee of any other person firm or company directly or indirectly any person firm or company who shall have been a client of the Firm [other than a client personally introduced by him or her to the Firm[41] and other

---

[39] This clause can give rise to difficulties. It must be made clear that a partner will not be indemnified against his or her own default. So a partner who defaults remains liable to indemnify his or her former partner against loss arising from that default. See comments as to negligence in Precedent 1: Standard Partnership Agreement, Clause T1.3 note 96, at p 56.

[40] These restrictions are by way of guidance only. Careful consideration must be given in each case having regard to the size of the firm, its business, its location and the other factors taken into account when considering the enforceability of restrictive covenants.

[41] Disputes can arise over introductions of business unless the firm has a well-settled procedure for identifying them.

than his or her relatives or a company wholly owned or controlled by him or her or his or her relatives] at any time during a period of 3 years immediately preceding the date when he or she ceased to be a Partner

T10.2   during a period of 3 years from the date of ceasing to be a Partner carry on or be concerned or engaged or interested whether directly or indirectly and whether by himself or herself or as a partner or employee of any other person firm or company in the [practice or profession of *or* business of . . .] within a radius of [one mile] from any address at which at the date of his or her ceasing to be a partner the Firm shall be carrying on the Partnership business

T10.3   at any time after ceasing to be a Partner and in any place carry on business under any style or name which shall include or refer to the Firm Name

T10.4   at any time suggest or cause to be suggested to any member of the Firm's staff that he or she might leave the employment of the Firm to work for the former Partner or for any company or firm with which the former Partner is or intends to be connected

T11   SEVERANCE OF RESTRICTIONS
It is hereby declared that the provisions of each of Clauses T10.1 to T10.4 respectively are intended to be read and construed independently of each other so that none of such separate provisions shall be dependent on any one or more of any of the other such provisions

T12   PAYMENT
T12.1   Annual Accounts shall be prepared at the Termination Date

T12.2   The Retirement Capital of the former Partner shall be repaid to him or her (or his or her personal representatives) by [6] equal [6-monthly] instalments the first of such instalments to be paid to him or her (or his or her personal representatives) [6] months after his or her Termination Date

T12.3   Retirement Interest calculated from the Termination Date shall be paid with each payment of his or her Retirement Capital

T13   TAX ELECTION[42]
T13.1   The former Partner shall if so requested in writing by the remaining Partner join in giving to H.M. Inspector of Taxes or any other requisite authority in such form as may be required any notice and join in making any election or the withdrawal or amendment thereof relating to any fiscal

[42] This clause is drafted to deal with firms which still have the opportunity to make a continuation election under the old Income and Corporation Taxes Act 1988, s 113 (see Appendix). (These are firms which commenced trade before 6 April 1994 and which have not decided to adopt an actual basis of taxation.) The clause can be deleted for firms which are under the new tax rules for partnerships (under the Finance Act 1994, s 215 replacing the Income and Corporation Taxes Act 1988, s 111) at the time of signature of the Agreement and which have no 'open' years on the old basis.

matter in connection with the affairs of the Partnership and for this purpose shall sign any such document and do any such act and provide any such information as shall be necessary to give effect to such Resolution[43]

T13.2 The remaining Partner shall indemnify the former Partner and his or her estate and effects from and against any taxation of whatsoever nature suffered by him or her or his or her estate as a result of ceasing to be a Partner in excess of what would have been suffered by such former Partner or his or her estate and effects had such notice or election or withdrawal or amendment thereof (as the case may be) not been given

T14 RETENTIONS

Sums retained from Retirement Capital for income tax which are not required to satisfy such Partner's share of any income tax assessments shall be credited to the Partner's Retirement Capital (or paid to him or her if his or her Retirement Capital has been repaid) as soon as the relevant income tax assessment has been agreed with the Inland Revenue and any deficiency in any sum so retained shall be reimbursed by the former Partner on demand

Part 3
Winding up

T15 DISTRIBUTION OF NET ASSETS

Upon the dissolution of the Partnership the assets and credits shall be sold or realised as soon as practicable and the proceeds applied

T15.1 first in paying and discharging the debts and liabilities of the Partnership and the expenses of and incidental to the winding up of the affairs of the Partnership any deficiency being contributed rateably by the Partners in the proportions in which they shared profits[44] immediately prior to dissolution

T15.2 second in repaying to the Partners rateably their Capital Accounts but so that no payment shall be made to a Partner whose Capital Account is less than his or her due proportion until repayments of Capital Account to other Partners have reduced their Capital Accounts to a similar proportional level

---

[43] Under the 'old' regime, unless an election is made under the Income and Corporation Taxes Act 1988, s 113 the firm has a 'cessation' for tax purposes on a partner leaving or joining the firm. A cessation is the 'default' position and so the indemnity is given if there is a continuation. However, if profits are reducing, a partner who leaves may have an additional tax liability if no election to continue is made.

[44] Note that profit shares determine the charge of any deficiency and the distribution of any surplus on dissolution. Consideration should be given to amending these clauses if capital shares differ from profit shares.

T15.3   third in paying any surplus rateably to the Partners in the proportions in
           which they shared profits[45] immediately prior to dissolution

T16   RESTRICTION ON USE OF FIRM'S NAME
           Neither Partner shall be entitled to practise after the date of dissolution
           under the Firm Name unless and to the extent that he or she shall have
           been authorised to do so by the other Partner[46]

---

[45]   See note 44 above.
[46]   This may prevent a partner trading under his or her own name after a dissolution.

SCHEDULE X

Execution

This Deed is intended to be delivered by each Partner on the date of delivery opposite that Partner's name

Name of Partner	Signature as a Deed	Signature of Witness
[name (1)]	....	....
[name (2)]	....	....

PRECEDENT 4: TRADING FIRM PARTNERSHIP AGREEMENT WITH OPTION FOR A SINGLE PARTNER TO CONTINUE

CONTENTS

PRECEDENT 4: TRADING FIRM PARTNERSHIP AGREEMENT WITH OPTION FOR A SINGLE PARTNER TO CONTINUE[1]

THIS PARTNERSHIP AGREEMENT[2] executed as a Deed[3] constitutes the terms on which the Partners have agreed to carry on business in partnership as [*trade or profession*] and is intended to be known as

'THE [*name of firm*] 199[. . .] PARTNERSHIP AGREEMENT'[4]

1.   THE SCHEDULES
           This Agreement includes the following Schedules and Tables:

Schedule D[5]	which contains **D**issolution provisions
Schedule F	which contains **F**inancial provisions
Table F	which contains details of capital profit shares and drawings
Schedule I	which contains **I**nterpretation of this Agreement and definitions used in this Agreement
Schedule M	which contains **M**eetings procedure and voting and management arrangements
Table M	which contains details of voting percentages
Schedule P	which contains **P**artners' names and addresses
Schedule T	which contains **T**ermination and payment provisions
Schedule X	which contains e**X**ecution of this Agreement by the Partners

---

[1] This precedent is designed for a small trading partnership in which there are some sleeping partners (called investing partners) and some working partners. The investing partners have no right to take part in the day-to-day running of the firm, and there is provision for appointment of a managing partner with similar authority to that of a managing director in a limited company, and for payment of partners' salaries. It also assumes that not all of the partners will work full time in the business and contains provision for payments for goodwill on a partner leaving.

    If there are to be no investing partners, the precedent can easily be amended by deletion of the references to 'Investing Partners' and 'Working Partners'.

[2] See 'About the Precedents' in the Introduction which describes the numbering system used in the precedents. First-time users of this precedent should read Schedule I (Interpretation) first.

[3] The Agreement is executed as a deed (Schedule X) to give effect to the following clauses:

    4.3   indemnity as to private debts;

    5.2   trust of property (desirable not essential);

    5.3   property indemnity;

    F7.3 and F7.4 tax indemnities.

[4] As the Agreement may initially be executed by partners on different days, and subsequently amended and executed by new partners, it is identified by a name, and not dated. See 'About the Precedents' in the Introduction and the Partnership Act 1890, s 19 (see Appendix) as to variation of partnership deeds.

[5] See note 2 above.

2.   DURATION – FIRM NAME

2.1   The Partnership shall continue until terminated in accordance with the provisions of this Agreement

2.2   The Partnership shall be carried on under the Firm Name or such other name or names as the Partners shall Resolve[6]

3.   CHANGES OF PARTNERS[7]

3.1   No person shall be admitted as a Partner otherwise than by a Resolution of the Partners in favour of the introduction of the new Partner and the terms of the introduction

3.2   Any person becoming a Partner shall signify his or her acceptance of this Agreement by signing as a Deed in Schedule X opposite the entry of his or her name and the relevant information relating to him or her shall be inserted in Schedule P

3.3   If any Partner shall cease to be a Partner then the Partnership shall not be dissolved as to the other Partners unless as a result thereof[8]

       3.3.1   there shall be no Working Partner in which event the Partnership shall be dissolved in accordance with Schedule D; or

       3.3.2   there shall be only one Partner who is a Working Partner in which event the Partnership shall be dissolved in accordance with Schedule D unless a Succession Notice shall be served

3.4   There shall be inserted in Schedule P against the entry of the name of any person who has ceased to be a Partner the date upon which he or she so ceased

4.   GENERAL DUTIES OF THE PARTNERS

4.1   Each Partner shall be just and faithful to the other Partners in all transactions dealings and matters relating to or affecting the Partnership and shall in all circumstances give a true and proper account thereof when reasonably required so to do by any of the other Partners

4.2   Each Partner shall devote the average number of working days per week in any period of 3 months to the business of the Firm as is set against that Partner's name in Schedule P and diligently and faithfully employ himself or herself therein and use his or her best endeavours to carry on the same for the utmost benefit of the Partnership[9]

---

[6]   'Resolve' and 'Resolution' are defined terms. See definitions in Schedule I at p 129 and Table M at p 133.

[7]   In many family partnerships, provisions are suggested that a partner can be introduced by a departing partner – sometimes nominated by will. I consider such provisions undesirable as partners should only ever be admitted to a firm with the consent of the other partners.

[8]   This clause causes a dissolution if no working partner remains, even if there is more than one investing partner, on the basis that the investing partners will not be in a position to carry on the business. It also gives a right for a sole partner who is a working partner to acquire the business. Careful consideration should be given to the desirability of such arrangements. See Schedule T at p 137 for the circumstances in which this might arise.

[9]   There is no requirement under the Partnership Act 1890 for any partner to devote any specific amount of time to the firm's business.

4.3 Each Partner shall at all times duly and punctually pay and discharge his or her separate and private debts and engagements whether present or future and keep the property of the Partnership and the other Partners and their personal representatives estates and effects indemnified therefrom and from all actions proceedings costs claims and demands in respect thereof

5. PARTNERSHIP PROPERTY

5.1 The Partnership shall be carried on at [*address* and at] such places as the Partners shall Resolve

5.2 The leases of any premises from time to time used for the purpose of the Partnership and property or securities or other assets of whatsoever kind held by the Partnership at the date hereof or hereafter acquired on behalf of the Partnership shall be the property of the Partnership and shall be held by such of the Partners in whose names the same may from time to time be vested in trust for the Partners in the shares in which they are from time to time entitled to share in capital

5.3 The Partners hereby indemnify any Partner or former Partner in whose name any such property or securities or other assets as aforesaid are for the time being vested (or have previously been vested) against all claims for rent property taxes costs of repairs alterations or improvements and insurance relating to any such property and generally in respect of any obligations in respect of any such property securities or other assets[10]

6. HOLIDAYS AND INCAPACITY

6.1 Each Working Partner shall be entitled (in addition to statutory holidays) to such period of holiday in each calendar year as is set against that Partner's name in Schedule P or to such other period as the Partners may from time to time Resolve

6.2 Without prejudice to the provisions of Clause T2 any Working Partner who shall be incapacitated (except by reason of pregnancy)[11] from carrying out his or her duties for the total number of working days set against that Partner's name in Schedule P[12] in any period of [18 months] shall be automatically suspended from acting as a Partner until he or she shall be certified by a doctor as fit to resume full-time work and shall have resumed his or her duties

7. RESTRICTIONS
Subject to the provisions of this Agreement and unless otherwise Resolved no Partner shall:

---

[10] Although such an indemnity is implied, an express indemnity is better. As a result of the recession in the early 1990s, a number of ex-partners have found themselves being sued on leases they signed for their firms many years ago, often without any formal documentation still in existence to prove their indemnity rights. Put a copy of your Partnership Agreement with your will!

[11] Consideration should be given to specific pregnancy leave. See Precedent 1: Standard Partnership Agreement, Clause 6.3 at p 28.

[12] Quote periods of absence in working days rather than months.

7.1   engage directly or indirectly in any other business in competition with that of the Firm

7.2   engage or (except for gross misconduct) dismiss any member of the staff of the Firm

7.3   employ any of the money goods or effects of the Firm or pledge the credit thereof except in the ordinary course of business and upon the account or for the benefit of the Firm

7.4   buy order or contract for any goods articles or property on behalf of the Firm in excess of [£1,000] in any one transaction

7.5   enter into any bond or become bail surety or security with or for any person or do or knowingly cause or suffer to be done anything whereby the Partnership property or any part thereof may be seized attached or taken in execution[13]

7.6   assign mortgage or charge his or her share in the Partnership or any part of such share

[8.   PREVIOUS AGREEMENTS
             Save in respect of continuing obligations to former Partners the previous Partnership Agreement dated [. . .] [(as varied by Resolution)] shall forthwith cease to have effect]

9.   VARIATION OF AGREEMENT
9.1   Subject as herein otherwise expressly provided the terms and provisions of this Agreement relating to financial matters (including by way of example but not of limitation shares of profit contributions to capital and repayment of capital) or voting rights may be varied by Resolution of the Partners

9.2   Subject as herein otherwise expressly provided any other terms and conditions of this Agreement may also be varied by Resolution of the Partners

9.3   No variation pursuant to this Clause shall take effect so as to prejudice the rights of any former Partner

9.4   Upon any variation of this Agreement amendments shall be made to the relevant page or pages or a new page or new pages shall be inserted in the Agreement and in either case shall be signed by [any 2 Partners]. A copy

---

[13] Another aspect of the unlimited liability of partners is that the firm is at risk of having its assets attacked if a partner does not meet his or her personal obligations. This clause would give grounds for expulsion if the firm's assets were attacked by a partner's creditors. Expulsion would not necessarily be justified if there was no real risk to the firm.

of the page or pages as amended or substituted shall be supplied to each Partner as soon as practical after signature[14]

10.   GENERAL

10.1   Save as herein otherwise provided all disputes and questions whatsoever which shall either during the Partnership or afterwards arise between the Partners or their respective personal representatives shall be referred to a single arbitrator who shall be appointed by the Partners involved in the dispute if they can agree upon one or (failing agreement) by the President for the time being of the Law Society on the application of any Partner or personal representative and in either case in accordance with and subject to the provisions of the Arbitration Acts 1950 to 1979[15]

10.2   Any notice authorised or required to be given or served by this Agreement shall be deemed to be duly served if the same shall be delivered personally to the person to whom it is intended to be given or shall be sent by post in a pre-paid letter sent by recorded delivery or by registered post and addressed to him or her at his or her last known place of abode in England and where so sent shall be deemed to be served on the first working day of the Firm which shall follow the day on which such letter would in the ordinary course of post have been delivered

10.3   A notice to the Partners shall be properly served if delivered to or served upon any [2] Partners in accordance with this Clause

[14]   This clause gives effect to the loose-leaf principles of this form of Agreement. This Agreement will be executed with one master copy and copies held by partners in a ring binder which can be updated as appropriate. I recommend that each page of the original document should be initialled by one partner for identification purposes. It is recommended that original pages which are amended are retained with the master copy. See 'About the Precedents' in the Introduction and Partnership Act 1890, s 19.

[15]   Partnership disputes before the courts should be avoided. Arbitration is a most suitable procedure for partners. Some firms name the arbitrator in their Agreement, often their solicitor.

SCHEDULE D

Dissolution Provisions

D1   **DISSOLUTION**
The Partnership may be dissolved by a Resolution[16] of the Partners and shall be dissolved in accordance with Clause 3.3

D2   **DISTRIBUTION OF NET ASSETS**
Upon the dissolution of the Partnership the assets and credits shall be sold or realised as soon as practicable and the proceeds applied

D2.1   first in paying and discharging the debts and liabilities of the Partnership and the expenses of and incidental to the winding up of the affairs of the Partnership any deficiency being contributed rateably by the Partners in the proportions in which they shared second shares of profits (as set out in Schedule F)[17] immediately prior to dissolution

D2.2   second in paying to those Partners who have made Tax Reserves the amount of such Tax Reserves [together with interest accrued on such Tax Reserves] in accordance with Clause F7.1 up to the date of dissolution and as between such Partners rateably according to the total of such Tax Reserves

D2.3   third in repaying to the Partners rateably their Capital Accounts but so that no payment shall be made to a Partner whose Capital Account is less than his or her due proportion until repayments of Capital Account to other Partners have reduced their Capital Accounts to a similar proportional level

D2.4   fourth in paying any surplus rateably to the Partners in the proportions in which they shared second shares of profits (as set out in Schedule F)[18] immediately prior to dissolution

D3   **EXECUTION OF DOCUMENTS**
The Partners respectively shall execute do or concur in all necessary or proper instruments acts matters and things for effecting or facilitating the getting in sale and realisation of the assets and credits of the Partnership and the due application and division of the proceeds thereof and for their mutual release or indemnity or otherwise

---

[16]   'Resolve' and 'Resolution' are defined terms. See definitions in Schedule I at p 129 and Table M at p 123.

[17]   Note that profit shares determine the contribution to any deficiency and the distribution of any surplus on dissolution. Consideration should be given to amending these clauses if capital shares differ from profit shares.

[18]   See note 17 above.

D4   RESTRICTION ON USE OF FIRM'S NAME
          No Partner shall be entitled to carry on business after the date of
          dissolution under the Firm Name unless and to the extent that he or she
          shall have been authorised to do so by all of the other Partners

SCHEDULE F

Financial Provisions

F1   CAPITAL[19]

F1.1   The capital of the Partnership shall be the amount[20] contributed as set out in Table F or such other amount as the Partners shall Resolve;[21]

F1.2   Any further capital required by the Partnership shall be contributed by the Partners in the proportions in which they are entitled to share in second shares of profits (as set out in this Schedule)[22]

F2   PROFIT SHARES

F2.1   The profits of the Partnership [after payment of interest pursuant to Clause F7.1] shall be divided between the Partners first in the first shares set out against the name of each Partner in Table F and second in the second shares set out against the name of each Partner in Table F subject to the provisions of this Clause[23]

F2.2   If in any Accounting Period the profits shall be insufficient to pay the first shares the deficiency shall be carried forward and be a first charge on the profits of the Firm for the succeeding Accounting Period

F2.3   In respect of a Working Partner who is incapacitated from carrying out his or her duties for the period set out in Clause 6.2 the profit share due to such Partner shall cease to accrue to such Partner from the end of such period of incapacity until he or she shall have resumed his or her duties in accordance with Clause 6.2

F3   DRAWINGS
        Each Partner shall be at liberty to draw out for his or her separate use on account of his or her accruing profit share for the then current Accounting Period the monthly amount set against his or her name in Table F[24]

---

[19] Partners are not entitled to interest on capital before signature of the Firm's Accounts (Partnership Act 1890, s 24(4)). Inequality of contribution can be dealt with by adjusting first shares of profits.

[20] See note 29 below as to reserves.

[21] 'Resolve' and 'Resolution' are defined terms. See definitions in Schedule I at p 129 and Table M at p 133.

[22] Initial contributions to capital will probably be unequal, but further capitalisation could be pro rata to second shares of profits.

[23] If it is desired to provide for pre-agreed increasing shares of profit in each year, a series of Tables F can be attached to the Agreement.

[24] It is a good discipline to establish fixed drawing limits for partners as a protection against overdrawing. In the absence of agreement, partners are not allowed drawings until after the signature of the annual accounts.

F4   MOTOR VEHICLES [AND BENEFITS]²⁵

Unless otherwise Resolved each Working Partner shall be provided with a motor vehicle up to a value of £[. . .] for use in connection with the Firm's business and the Firm will pay the cost of road fund service repair insurance and for all running expenses (including fuel) in connection with business use. Motor vehicles will be replaced after [4] years or [80,000] miles whichever occurs first

F5   ANNUAL ACCOUNTS
F5.1   The Annual Accounts shall be prepared as soon as practical after each Accounting Date by reference to generally accepted accounting principles

F5.2   The Annual Accounts shall be signed by all the Partners and when so signed shall be binding on all the Partners except that if any manifest error therein be detected within 6 months after such signature such error shall be rectified immediately

F5.3   The Annual Accounts shall be prepared on the basis that (unless otherwise Resolved²⁶):
    F5.3.1   the goodwill of the Partnership shall be treated as having no value and the value thereof (if any) shall not feature therein
    F5.3.2   the Annual Accounts for each Accounting Period shall be prepared on a consistent basis with the previous Annual Accounts (if any)
    [F5.3.3   stock shall be valued at the lower of cost or net realisable value]²⁷

F6   DISTRIBUTION OF PROFITS
F6.1   The profits of the Partnership in each Accounting Period after taking into account drawings and such reserves as shall be Resolved upon by the Partners on the advice of the Partnership Accountants²⁸ (including the reserves referred to in Clause F7.1) shall be divided between the Partners immediately after they have signed the Annual Accounts in respect of that Accounting Period²⁹

---

²⁵ Insert at the end of this clause any benefits which partners are to enjoy and which they wish to have recorded in the Agreement eg BUPA, Life Insurance, Permanent Health Insurance etc.

²⁶ See note 56 below.

²⁷ Insert any other special accounting requirements particular to the business.

²⁸ Clearly, advice will be taken from the partnership accountants in relation to tax reserves, but this clause is a reminder that other reserves may cause some contention between partners – eg a sinking fund for building refurbishment or purchase. The issue should be considered in connection with Clause F1.1, as a permanent requirement for reserve should be dealt with as an increase in capital. This clause *obliges* the partners to obtain advice from the accountants, which can take the heat out of the argument.

²⁹ A reminder that partners are entitled to draw their surplus profits after signature of the accounts. If the partnership cannot afford a run on its bank account, then the partners should decide to reserve or increase capital.

F6.2   If it shall appear at any time that any Partner has drawn out more than the amount of drawings authorised pursuant to Clause F3 or (subject to Clause F2.2) more than his or her profit share in respect of any Accounting Period that Partner shall forthwith repay the deficiency to the Partnership and until such repayment the amount of such deficiency shall be a first charge on and be set off against future drawings [and shall bear interest[30] at [2 per cent per annum over the base rate for the time being of the Firm's bankers calculated with 3-monthly rests][31] from the last day of that Accounting Period until repayment][32]

F7   TAXATION[33]

F7.1   In respect of each Accounting Period [to which Section 215 of the Finance Act 1994 applies] the Partners shall Resolve upon the amount of income tax which they estimate [on the advice of the Partnership Accountants][34] to be payable by each Partner in respect of such period[35] and which they shall transfer to Tax Reserve in respect of each Partner. Each such reserve shall be retained until an assessment to income tax is made upon the relevant Partner and the amount of the assessment (or so much thereof as is represented by the reserve) shall be paid to H.M. Collector of Taxes on the date when the assessment is due for payment. Any surplus of the reserve made in respect of that assessment shall thereupon be repaid to the relevant Partner and any deficiency shall be provided by the relevant Partner out of his or her own resources. Such reserves shall carry interest at [the base rate for the time being of the Firm's bankers calculated with 3-monthly rests][36] from the date of the Resolution until payment (or at such other rate and on such other basis as may be determined by a Resolution of the Partners)

---

[30] As partners are not normally entitled to interest on capital (see note 19 above), it may be appropriate to charge interest to overdrawn partners.

[31] The rate at which the firm borrows money from its bank would seem appropriate.

[32] Partners in smaller firms frequently leave excess capital (or undrawn profits) in the firm. In such event, consideration should be given to introducing the concept of advances as in Schedule F in Precedent 1: Standard Partnership Agreement, see p 38.

[33] This clause is drafted to deal with both new tax rules for partnerships under the Finance Act 1994, s 215 (replacing the Income and Corporation Taxes Act 1988, s 111) (see Appendix) and also firms which still have the opportunity to make a continuation election under the old Income and Corporation Taxes Act 1988, s 113. (These are firms which commenced trade before 6 April 1994 and which have not decided to adopt an actual basis of taxation.) For firms which are on the new basis at the time of signature of the Agreement and which have no 'open' years on the old basis, the words in brackets in the first two lines of Clause F7.1 and Clauses F7.2 to F7.4 can be deleted. See heading 'Taxation' in 'About the Law' in the Introduction.

[34] See note 28 above.

[35] Even though the partners have no joint liability for income tax under the new rules, it is considered desirable not to permit partners to draw against profits on the basis that they will settle their own tax when the bill arrives. For some partners, the temptation to spend the apparent extra income may be difficult to resist. Most existing firms already reserve for tax and most existing partners will be prepared to accept a continuation of present practice. In most firms, the partnership accountants will continue to prepare the tax computations.

[36] A rate should be selected which encourages partners to leave capital with the firm and which has some advantage to the firm as well. Base rate seems appropriate.

F7.2   Upon or after any Partner ceasing to be a Partner [(unless by reason thereof the Partnership shall be dissolved)][37] and upon or after the admission of any new Partner all Partners (including a new Partner and any former Partner and the personal representatives of any deceased Partner) shall if so Resolved by the Partners join in giving to H.M. Inspector of Taxes or any other requisite authority in such form as may be required any notice and join in making any election or the withdrawal or amendment thereof relating to any fiscal matter in connection with the affairs of the Partnership and for this purpose shall sign any such document and do any such act and provide any such information as shall be necessary to give effect to such Resolution. The Partners may Resolve to nominate a Partner to sign such document on behalf of some or all of the Partners[38]

F7.3   The Partners shall indemnify any former Partner and his or her estate and effects from and against any taxation of whatsoever nature suffered by him or her or his or her estate as a result of ceasing to be a Partner in excess of what would have been suffered by such former Partner or his or her estate and effects had such notice or election or withdrawal or amendment thereof (as the case may be) not been given

[F7.4   The Partners (other than the new Partner to whom the indemnity is given) shall indemnify any new Partner from and against any taxation of whatsoever nature suffered in excess of what would have been suffered by such new Partner as a result of his or her admission as a Partner had such notice or election or withdrawal or amendment thereof (as the case may be) not been given][39]

F8   BOOKS OF ACCOUNT
        All proper and usual books of account and entries therein shall be kept (in either paper or electronic form) by the Partners and each Partner shall ensure that full and proper entries are duly and punctually made of all business transacted by him or her or at his or her direction on account of the Firm

F9   BANKING
F9.1   The Firm shall maintain bank accounts with such bankers as the Partners shall from time to time Resolve

F9.2   All Partnership monies (not required for current expenses) and securities for monies shall as and when received be paid into or deposited with the Firm's bankers for the credit of the Firm's accounts. All cheques on such

---

[37]   Delete if there will never be less than three partners.
[38]   Under the 'old' regime, unless an election is made under the Income and Corporation Taxes Act 1988, s 113, the firm has a 'cessation' for tax purposes on a partner leaving or joining the firm. A cessation is the 'default' position and so the indemnity is given if there is a continuation. However, if profits are reducing a partner who leaves may have an additional tax liability if no election to continue is made.
[39]   Many firms do not consider it appropriate to give this indemnity to an incoming partner.

accounts shall be drawn by any [one Working Partner *or* the Managing Partner] in respect of amounts under [£1,000] for any one payee and by any [2] Partners in respect of amounts of [£1,000] or over unless otherwise Resolved by the Partners

TABLE F[40]

Capital Contributions Profit Shares and Drawings

Capital contributions[41] profit shares[42] and drawings[43] with effect from the [. . .] day of [. . .] 199[. . .] shall be as follows:

Partner	Capital	First shares of profits[44]	Second shares of profits	Monthly drawings
[name (1)]	£	£	[. . .]%	£
[name (2)]	£	£	[. . .]%	£
[name (3)]	£	£	[. . .]%	£
[name (4)]	£	£	[. . .]%	£
Total	£	£	100%	£

---

[40] Tables are placed on separate pages for ease of replacement. See note 14 above.
[41] See Clause F1 at p 122.
[42] See Clause F2 at p 122.
[43] See Clause F3 at p 122.
[44] This column is expressed in amounts rather than percentages to allow for partners' salaries which are commonly used in trading partnerships.

SCHEDULE I

Interpretation and Definitions

I1   DEFINITIONS
        In this Agreement the following expressions shall where the context so
        admits have the following meanings

'Accounting Date'	the date up to which the Annual Accounts are drawn and until otherwise Resolved[45] the [. . .] day of [. . .] in each year
'Annual Accounts'	the accounts drawn in accordance with Schedule F
'Accounting Period'	the period from one Accounting Date to the next Accounting Date
'Capital Account'	in relation to any Partner his or her share of the capital of the Partnership in accordance with Clause F1
'Eligible Votes'[46]	the votes of all Partners whether or not attending a meeting except a Partner disqualified from voting pursuant to Clause M2.2
'Firm'	the business carried on by the Partners in partnership under the Firm Name pursuant to this Agreement
'Firm Name'	[X Y and Z] or any colourable imitation thereof or any combination of names which include any or all of [X Y or Z] or any colourable imitation of any such respective names
'Investing Partners'	the persons whose names are set out in Part 2 of Schedule P
'Managing Partner'	the Partner appointed in accordance with Clause M4
'Partners'	the Investing Partners and the Working Partners and where the context so admits such of them as shall continue to

---

[45] 'Resolve' and 'Resolution' are defined terms. See definitions in this Schedule and Table M at
p 133.
[46] This definition needs careful consideration. Is voting by:
   1   all Partners?; or
   2   all Partners who attend a meeting?; and
   3   votes by percentage of capital or votes allocated per partner?

	be Partners in the Partnership and any other future Partners for the time being but not any salaried partners
'the Partnership'	the partnership [presently subsisting *or* created hereby] between the Partners including any partnership which is a successor to that partnership under whatever name
'Partnership Accountants'	Messrs [. . .] or such other chartered accountants as the Partners shall Resolve
'Resolve' and 'Resolution'	to determine in accordance with Schedule M
'Retirement Capital'	a sum equal to the amount of capital standing to the credit of a Partner in his or her Capital Account on his or her Termination Date after adding his or her profit share (after actual drawings) from the previous Accounting Date until his or her Termination Date and after deducting therefrom

1. (if the Partner shall have been expelled from the Partnership pursuant to Clause T3) such sum as the remaining Partners shall Resolve to be necessary or sufficient to discharge all or any liability of the Partnership directly or indirectly attributable to the conduct of the Partner

[2. such sum as [in the opinion of the Partnership Accountants] may be required to satisfy his or her share of any income tax assessment which may be made upon the Partnership for any year of assessment ended prior to his or her Termination Date; and

3. the appropriate proportion of his or her share of any income tax assessment for the year of assessment in which he or she ceases to be a Partner][47]

---

[47]   For firms which are on the new tax rules for partnerships under the Finance Act 1994, s 215 (replacing the Income and Corporation Taxes Act 1988, s 111) (see Appendix) at the time of signature of the Agreement and which have no 'open' years on the old basis, the words in brackets can be deleted. See note 33 above.

'Retirement Interest'	interest at [... per cent per annum above the base rate of [...] Bank plc from time to time] computed with [6-monthly] rests[48]
'Succession Notice'	a notice in writing pursuant to Clause T4
'Table F'	the table at the end of Schedule F
'Table M'	the table at the end of Schedule M
'Tax Reserve'	the amount standing to the credit of a Partner in the books of the Partnership for that Partner's reserve for taxation pursuant to Clause F7.1
'Termination Date'	the date on which a Partner ceases to be a Partner whether pursuant to this Agreement or by death
'Working Partners'	the persons whose names are set out in Part 1 of Schedule P

I2   INTERPRETATION

I2.1   Headings to Clauses and Schedules are for ease of reference only and shall be of no effect in construing the provisions of this Agreement

I2.2   Where the context so admits:

I2.2.1   words importing the singular number shall include the plural and words importing the plural number shall include the singular

I2.2.2   references to statutes or to sections of statutes shall include any statutory modifications or re-enactments thereof for the time being in force

---

[48]   The interest rate could be the same as the rate at which the firm borrows funds from its bankers. There is no reason for the firm to profit from the capital of a retired partner, although its retention will help cash flow.

SCHEDULE M

Meetings Voting and Management

M1   **PARTNERS' MEETINGS**
     The Partners shall meet for the purpose of dealing with Partnership matters at times and dates of which at least [one week's][49] notice shall be given by any Partner to all Partners (except in case of emergency)

M2   **VOTES AND VOTING RESTRICTIONS**
M2.1 On any proposed Resolution a partner shall be entitled to the number of votes set against his or her name in Schedule P

M2.2 A Partner shall not be entitled to vote on a Resolution:[50]
     M2.2.1 for his or her election as Managing Partner pursuant to Clause M4.1
     M2.2.2 to change his or her authority as Managing Partner pursuant to Clause M4.2
     M2.2.3 to cause his or her retirement by reason of incapacity pursuant to Clause T2
     M2.2.4 to expel him or her pursuant to Clause T3

M3   **VOTING PERCENTAGES**
M3.1 For a Resolution to be passed arising under the Clause set out in column 1 of Table M a brief description of which (for convenience and not by way of construction) is set out in column 2 of Table M the percentage of Eligible Votes[51] set out in column 3 of Table M must be in favour of the Resolution

M3.2 Notwithstanding Clause M3.1 for any Resolution to be passed a majority of the Eligible Votes of both the Investing Partners and of the Working Partners shall be in favour of the Resolution

M3.3 All decisions of the Partners which do not arise under any Clause shall be made by Resolution

M4   **MANAGEMENT**[52]
M4.1 The Partners (excluding the Partner proposed for election) may Resolve that a Partner be elected to the office of Managing Partner. Such Partner

---

[49] The period and formalities of notice will vary according to the size of the firm and the location of its premises.

[50] 'Resolve' and 'Resolution' are defined terms. See definitions in Schedule I at p 129 and Table M at p 133.

[51] Careful consideration needs to be given to this definition.

[52] All of these suggested provisions are likely to need careful consideration.

shall be elected for a term of [3] years and may be re-elected [once]. The Managing Partner at the date hereof is [*name*] whose term of office expires on [. . .] and who is [not] eligible for re-election

M4.2   Until otherwise Resolved by the Partners (excluding the Managing Partner) the Managing Partner shall have day to day authority to manage the business of the Partnership on behalf of the Partners[53]

M4.3   Investing Partners may attend and vote at meetings of the Partners but shall otherwise have no authority to enter into any obligation on behalf of the Firm, nor to take part in the management of the business of the Firm

---

[53] The managing partner's authority may need to be carefully defined.

TABLE M[54]

Voting Percentages

Clause	Brief description	Percentage of Eligible Votes[55]
2.2	Change Firm Name	[51]
3.1	Admit new Partner	[100]
5.1	Change Partnership premises	[75]
6.1	Change holiday entitlement	[51]
7	Waive restrictions	[75]
9.1	Vary Agreement – financial/voting	[100]
9.2	Vary Agreement – other	[51]
D1	Dissolve Partnership	[100]
F1.1	Fix Partnership capital	[100]
F4	Vary motor vehicle provisions	[75]
F5.3	Change accounting basis[56]	[100]
F6.1	Agree reserves	[75]
F7.1	Estimate Tax Reserves	[75]
F7.1	Vary interest on Tax Reserves	[75]
F7.2	Sign tax election	[75]
F9.1	Change bank	[51]
F9.2	Change bank mandate	[51]
I1	Change Accounting Date[57]	[100]

[54]   Tables are placed on separate pages for ease of replacement. See Clause 9.4 at p 118 and note 14 above.

[55]   All of the percentages in this Table are merely suggestions.

[56]   This resolution may well have the effect of penalising a partner on changes in shares, or retirement. For example, a decision to change the basis of stock valuation, or to change the basis of depreciation, will have the effect of altering the profits which arise in that accounting period.

[57]   100% is suggested for changing the accounting date as it may have implications for profit shares (if shares change at the end of an accounting period), and also for retirement date.

Clause		Brief description	Percentage of Eligible Votes
I1		Change Partnership Accountants	[51]
M3.3		Resolution not varying the Agreement	[51]
M4.1	★	Elect Managing Partner	[51]
M4.2	★	Change Managing Partner's authority	[51]
T2	★	Retire Partner for incapacity	[100]
T3	★	Expel Partner	[100]

★ Clause M2 restricts entitlement to vote on these Resolutions

Clause M3.2 provides that all Resolutions require a majority of both Investing and Working Partners

SCHEDULE P

The Partners

Part 1 Working Partners

Name and address	Identifying initials	Working days per week	Holidays days per year	Incapacity days per year	No of votes	Date joined	Date ceased

Part 2   Investing Partners

Name and address	Identifying initials	Working days per week	Holidays days per year	Incapacity days per year	No of votes	Date joined	Date ceased
		n/a	n/a	n/a			
		n/a	n/a	n/a			

SCHEDULE T
Termination and Repayment Provisions

Part 1
Termination[58]

T1   **RETIREMENT BY AGE OR NOTICE**

Each Working Partner shall retire on the Accounting Date following his or her [65th] birthday and each Partner may (if he or she shall give to the other Partners not less than [6] months' notice in writing of his or her intention to do so) retire from the Partnership on any Accounting Date

T2   **RETIREMENT DUE TO INCAPACITY**

If a Working Partner has been or in the view of competent medical opinion is likely to be incapacitated from carrying out his or her duties as a Partner for the total period set out in Clause 6.2 (and without prejudice to the provisions of Clause 6.2) then the Partners may Resolve[59] that such Partner shall retire from the Partnership on the date specified in the Resolution by reason of incapacity in which event he or she shall cease to be a Partner on such date

T3   **EXPULSION**

T3.1   If any Partner shall:

    T3.1.1 charge assign or transfer his or her share in the Partnership or any part thereof or suffer the same to be charged for his or her separate debt under the Partnership Act 1890

    T3.1.2 become bankrupt or insolvent or compound or make any arrangement with or for the benefit of his or her creditors or apply for an interim order pursuant to Section 253 of the Insolvency Act 1986 or have a petition for a bankruptcy order against him or her presented to the Court

    T3.1.3 act in any manner inconsistent with the good faith observable between Partners

    T3.1.4 be guilty of any conduct which would be a ground for dissolution of the Partnership by the Court

    T3.1.5 being a Working Partner absent himself or herself from the Partnership without proper cause for more than [4] weeks (consecutive or otherwise) in any period of 12 months[60]

---

[58] Consider whether a provision for compulsory retirement is appropriate to the firm. See Precedent 1: Standard Partnership Agreement, Clause T8 at p 60.

[59] 'Resolve' and 'Resolution' are defined terms. See definitions in Schedule I at p 129 and Table M at p 133.

[60] Even 4 weeks may be too long for unexplained absences.

T3.1.6 be convicted of any offence involving fraud or dishonesty or be sentenced to a term of imprisonment whether or not suspended

T3.1.7 be guilty of any conduct calculated or tending to injure the reputation of the Firm or likely to have a serious or adverse effect upon the Firm's business

T3.1.8 commit any substantial breach of this Agreement

then and in any such case the Partners may Resolve to determine the Partnership so far as it concerns such Partner on the date specified in the Resolution in which event he or she shall cease to be a Partner on such date

T3.2 If any question shall arise concerning the existence of the grounds for expulsion or exercise of the power to expel conferred by Clause T3.1 such question shall be referred to arbitration under the provisions of Clause 10.1

T4 SUCCESSION NOTICE[61]

T4.1 If, following termination, there shall be only one Partner who is a Working Partner, that Partner may

T4.1.1 within [one month] of receiving notice pursuant to clause T1;[62] or

T4.1.2 within [6] months prior to the Accounting Date following the other Working Partner's 65th birthday; or

T4.1.3 at the time of giving notice pursuant to clauses T2[63] or T3 or before the expiry thereof; or

T4.1.4 within [one month] of the date of death of the other Working Partner[64]

give a Succession Notice to the other Partner or Partners (or his or her or their personal representatives as the case may be)

T4.2 If a Succession Notice shall be served the Partner serving the Succession Notice shall acquire the share of the other Partner in accordance with Part 2 of this Schedule and Schedule D shall not apply

---

[61] See note 8 above.

[62] This can be a two-edged sword. On the one hand, it is not fair that a partner who wishes to continue should be forced to have a dissolution just because the other partner wishes to retire (or at least to have the threat of a dissolution used in negotiations). On the other hand, if two partners are in dispute, why should the one who resigns, possibly because he or she cannot stand the aggravation, be penalised by losing the business. This is an issue which should be brought to clients' attention so that they can decide!

[63] It is difficult to decide what is fair. Obviously, if a partner has been sick for some time it would be unfair for the continuing partner to be forced to have a dissolution of the firm. But is it fair to the sick partner that the other partner should be able to force a dissolution, with the attendant advantage in acquiring the business? Perhaps this option for a succession notice should be to allow *either* partner to require the healthy partner to continue.

[64] See note 63 above. Perhaps this should also be a two-way notice provision.

Part 2
Repayment and consequent provisions

[If, following termination, there shall be only one Partner who is a Working Partner, this Part of this Schedule shall only have effect if a Succession Notice shall have been served]

T5   GOODWILL[65]

T5.1   Any Partner ceasing to be a Partner shall be entitled to a payment in respect of his or her interest in the goodwill of the Partnership

T5.2   For the purpose of computing such payment the goodwill of the Partnership shall be valued as either:

     T5.2.1   the average of the total of the second shares of profits for the 2 Accounting Periods prior to the Termination Date and of the Accounting Period during which the Termination Date occurs (or ending with the Termination Date as the case may be); or (if there shall not have been 2 such prior Accounting Periods)

     T5.2.2   the total of the second shares of profits for the period from the commencement of the Partnership until the Accounting Date prior to the Termination Date (if any) and of the Accounting Period during which the Termination Date occurs (or ending with the Termination Date as the case may be)

T5.3   The amount of the payment to which the former Partner shall be entitled shall be the value of the goodwill calculated as set out in Clause T5.2 multiplied by the percentage of the second share of profit to which the former Partner would have been entitled if he or she had remained a Partner for the whole of the Accounting Period during which the Termination Date occurs

T5.4   The calculations set out in this Clause shall be made by the Partnership Accountants and certified by them to the Partners and the former Partner as soon as possible after the Termination Date and their certificate shall be final and binding on the parties

T6   PAYMENT
     Upon any Partner ceasing to be a Partner

[T6.1   any Tax Reserve held for him or her together with all accrued interest at his or her Termination Date shall be repaid to him or her or his or her personal representatives within [3] months from his or her Termination Date]

T6.2   the Retirement Capital of such Partner and the goodwill payment calculated in accordance with Clause T5 shall be repaid to him or her (or his or her personal representatives) by [6] equal [6-monthly] instalments

---

[65]   This calculation and the multiplier will vary in each individual case.

the first of such instalments to be paid to him or her (or his or her personal representatives) [6] months after his or her Termination Date

T6.3   Retirement Interest calculated from the Termination Date shall be paid with each payment of his or her Retirement Capital [and his or her Tax Reserve]

T7   **RETENTIONS**

Sums retained from Retirement Capital for income tax which are not required to satisfy a Partner's share of any income tax assessments shall be credited to the Partner's Retirement Capital (or paid to him or her if his or her Retirement Capital has been repaid) as soon as the relevant income tax assessment has been agreed with the Inland Revenue and any deficiency in any sum so retained shall be reimbursed by the Partner on demand

T8   **GENERAL PROVISIONS**

T8.1   Upon a Partner ceasing to be a Partner his or her profit shares shown in Table F shall be cancelled

T8.2   The remaining Partners shall succeed to all the interest of the former Partner in the Partnership (subject to his or her rights herein contained) [in the shares which as between themselves they share second shares of profits *or* equally][66] and shall undertake all the debts liabilities and obligations of the former Partner and will indemnify and keep the former Partner indemnified against all such debts liabilities and obligations other than such as are hereby deemed to be for his or her separate account or are directly or indirectly attributable to any act or omission of the former Partner but without prejudice to any subsisting liability of the former Partner for breach of this Agreement[67]

T8.3   If and so far as it shall be necessary to apportion profits and losses for any period the apportionment shall be on a time basis by reference to the then current Accounting Period

---

[66] Careful consideration needs to be given to this issue. Allocating a share equally between the remaining partners can help in a move towards equality of shares.

[67] This clause can give rise to difficulties.

First, it must be made clear that a partner will not be indemnified against his or her own default. So a partner who is expelled for cause remains liable to indemnify his former partners against loss arising from that default.

Second, a partner who is negligent remains liable to indemnify for his or her own negligence. This is not an issue if the firm has sufficient negligence insurance to cover a claim, as the insurance extends to all partners, including one who is negligent. Moreover, in most cases of negligence, the claim rarely arises exclusively from one person's mistake, making claims difficult to pursue inside a firm.

Third is the liability of all partners for negligence claims in excess of the firm's insurance cover. My view is that if such a claim has been intimated at the termination date, a reserve should be included in the retirement accounts, but, if not, the former partner should get a full indemnity against future claims, whenever the negligent act happened.

T8.4   A former Partner shall have no rights whatsoever against any remaining Partner save as herein expressly provided

T9   RESTRICTIONS[68]
A former Partner shall not:

T9.1   at any time solicit whether by himself or herself or as a partner or employee of any other person firm or company directly or indirectly any person firm or company who shall have been a customer of the Firm at any time during a period of 3 years immediately preceding the date when he or she ceased to be a Partner

T9.2   during a period of 3 years from the date of ceasing to be a Partner carry on or be concerned or engaged or interested whether directly or indirectly and whether by himself or herself or as a partner or employee of any other person firm or company in the [business of . . .] within a radius of [one mile] from any address at which at the date of his or her ceasing to be a partner the Firm shall be carrying on the Partnership business

T9.3   at any time after ceasing to be a Partner and in any place carry on business under any style or name which shall include or refer to the Firm Name

T9.4   at any time suggest or cause to be suggested to any member of the Firm's staff that he or she might leave the employment of the Firm to work for the former Partner or for any company or firm with which the former Partner is or intends to be connected

T10   SEVERANCE OF RESTRICTIONS
It is hereby declared that the provisions of each of Clauses T9.1 to T9.4 respectively are intended to be read and construed independently of each other so that none of such separate provisions shall be dependent on any one or more of any of the other such provisions

---

[68] These restrictions are by way of guidance only. Careful consideration must be given in each case having regard to the size of the firm, its business, its location and the other factors taken into account when considering the enforceability of restrictive covenants.

SCHEDULE X

Execution

This Deed is intended to be delivered by each Partner on the date of delivery opposite that Partner's name

Name of Partner	Signature as a Deed	Date of Delivery	Signature of Witness
[name (1)]	....		....
[name (2)]	....		....
[name (3)]	....		....
[name (4)]	....		....

PRECEDENT 5: CONSULTANCY LETTER[1]

[firm name
address
date]

[name of retiring partner
address]

Dear *[retiring partner]*

We confirm that the Firm wishes to retain your services as a consultant and this letter sets out the terms of the consultancy.

1.   The consultancy commences on *[date]* and continues until *[date or terminated by either of us giving [3] months' written notice of termination to the other]*.

2.   During the consultancy[2] you will be available to render such advice and assistance to the Firm as we shall request up to a maximum of [30] hours in any month.[3]

3.   We will pay you a consultancy fee at the rate of [£ . . .] per annum (plus VAT if applicable) by equal monthly payments in arrear.

4.   The consultancy fee will be reviewed annually in *[month]*.

5.   *[set out any commission or similar arrangements]*

6.   We will pay or reimburse to you the cost of *[set out expenses to be reimbursed by the firm]*.

7.   Your name will be printed on our notepaper as a consultant.

8.   This letter does not vary or waive any of the provisions of the Firm's Partnership Agreement to which you were a party affecting retiring partners.[4]

---

1   This letter is suitable for a retiring equity partner who will continue in a consultancy capacity with the firm. It is drafted on the assumption that there is a high degree of trust between the parties, and that the function of the letter is only to define key terms, and for evidential purposes. A more formal consultancy arrangement with an 'unknown' consultant should be viewed from a perspective of employment law rather than partnership law.

2   Specific duties can be set out in this clause.

3   If the consultant is to continue to enjoy self-employed status, the consultancy should not be full time and the consultant should not be restricted from undertaking other work (subject, of course to any restrictive covenants in the partnership agreement).

4   Some limited form of restrictive covenant could be inserted here.

9.   This letter does not create a partnership as between yourself and the Firm and as a consultant you have no authority to bind the Firm.

Please confirm your agreement to these terms by signing and returning the attached copy of this letter to me.

Yours sincerely
[*signature on behalf of firm*]

I confirm the above
[*signature of retiring partner*]
[*date*]

PRECEDENT 6:   MERGER AGREEMENT BETWEEN TWO PARTNERSHIPS

CONTENTS

PRECEDENT 6: MERGER AGREEMENT BETWEEN TWO PARTNERSHIPS

A MERGER AGREEMENT[1] dated the [. . .] day of [. . .] 199[. . .]
BETWEEN

(1) [ABC] PARTNERS

(2) [123] PARTNERS

for the merger of the Firms of [ABC] and [123]

1.	DEFINITIONS AND INTERPRETATION	
1.1	In this Agreement the following expressions shall where the context so admits have the following meanings	

'[ABC] Partners'	the persons whose names are set out in Schedule 1 who carry on business as [ABC] [*trade or profession*] from the [ABC] premises
'[123] Partners'	the persons whose names are set out in Schedule 2 who carry on business as [123] [*trade or profession*] from the [123] premises
'Accounting Date'	[*day prior to Merger Date*]
'Final Accounts'	the accounts to be prepared pursuant to Clause 7
'Firm Name'	[*new name*]
'Merger Date'	[*date*]
'New Firm'	the firm to be created pursuant to this Agreement
'Parties'	the parties to this Agreement
'Partners'	the [ABC] Partners and the [123] Partners and where the context so admits such of them as shall continue to be Partners in the New Firm and any other future Partners for the time being

1.2   Headings to Clauses and Schedules are for ease of reference only and shall be of no effect in construing the provisions of this Agreement

1.3   Where the context so admits:

---

[1] This is only an outline framework of a Merger Agreement. Many are documented by a new Partnership Agreement without a formal Merger Agreement. There are very few genuine mergers, most being takeovers dressed up as mergers and this draft assumes that one firm will be the dominant influence. The precedent for an Admission Deed may be more suitable in many instances.

1.3.1   words importing the singular number shall include the plural and words importing the plural number shall include the singular

1.3.2   references to statutes or to sections of statutes shall include any statutory modifications or re-enactments thereof for the time being in force

2.   CONDITIONS OF AGREEMENT

2.1   This Agreement is conditional upon compliance with the following conditions prior to the Merger Date:

[2.1.1 agreement between the Parties of a form of Partnership Agreement between them]

2.1.2   [*other conditions*]²

2.2   If any of the conditions set out in Clause 2.1 shall not have been complied with by [*date*] then either party may terminate this Agreement by written notice to the other

3.   FORMATION OF NEW FIRM

3.1   Subject to Clause 2 the existing partnerships of [ABC] Partners and [123] Partners shall terminate on the Accounting Date and the Partners shall enter into partnership as the New Firm on the Merger Date and carry on business thereafter under the Firm Name

3.2   The New Firm shall carry on business from all of the trading premises of the Parties

4.   PARTNERSHIP AGREEMENT

The New Firm's Partnership Agreement shall be in the form [of the ABC Partnership Agreement dated [*date*] with the amendments set out in Schedule 3 *or* annexed hereto *or* to be agreed pursuant to Clause 2]

5.   CAPITAL

5.1   The capital of the New Firm shall be the sum of [£ . . .] which shall be contributed as to [£ . . .] by the [ABC] Partners and as to [£ . . .] by the [123] Partners

5.1.1   The proportions in which as between themselves the [ABC] Partners shall contribute capital shall be the proportions in which they share profits in [ABC] at the Accounting Date or in such other proportions as they shall notify the [123] Partners prior to the Merger Date

5.1.2   The proportions in which as between themselves the [123] Partners shall contribute capital shall be the proportions in which they share profits in [123] at the Accounting Date or in such

---

² List other conditions precedent to completion. These might include due diligence in respect of accounts and negligence; negotiations with partners who do not wish to join; review of client lists and discussions with clients; client conflict of interest; pensions; cars; staff employment terms and so on. In practice, although these conditions are often set down in draft documents, mergers often happen first with the documentation being signed later – such is the nature of partnership.

other proportions as they shall notify the [ABC] Partners prior to the Merger Date

5.2 The opening capital of each Partner shall be the amount standing to the credit of his or her respective capital account in the Final Accounts

5.3 Any deficiency in the capital of any Partner shall be made up by him or her to the amount which he or she is required to contribute by [*date*] together with interest from the Merger Date at the rate of [*rate*]

5.4 Any surplus in the capital of any Partner may be withdrawn by him or her after [*date*] and shall be credited with interest from the Merger Date at the rate of [*rate*]

6. PROFIT SHARES
The profits of the New Firm shall be allocated as to [. . . %] to the [ABC] Partners and as to [. . . %] to the [123] Partners

6.1 The proportions in which as between themselves the [ABC] Partners shall share profits shall be the proportions in which they share profits in [ABC] at the Accounting Date or in such other proportions as they shall notify the [123] Partners prior to the Merger Date

6.2 The proportions in which as between themselves the [123] Partners shall share profits shall be the proportions in which they share profits in [123] at the Accounting Date or in such other proportions as they shall notify the [ABC] Partners prior to the Merger Date

7. ACCOUNTING
7.1 The [ABC] Partners in respect of [ABC] shall procure that [ABC] shall prepare accounts to the Accounting Date and the [123] Partners in respect of [123] shall procure that [123] shall prepare accounts to the Accounting Date for the purpose of the merger on the basis that both such accounts shall be consistent with each other

7.2 Work-in-progress shall be valued in a manner equivalent to that hitherto adopted by [ABC]

7.3 The New Firm's Accounting Date shall be [*date*]

8. SUBSISTING LIABILITIES
8.1 Save as set out in this clause the New Firm shall be liable for all of the liabilities (both actual and contingent) of [ABC] and [123] at the Merger Date

8.2 The [ABC] Partners or (as the case may be) the [123] Partners shall be responsible for and shall jointly and severally indemnify and keep indemnified the New Firm from and against all liabilities (both direct and indirect actual and contingent) in excess of [£ . . .] in the aggregate of their respective firms on or before the Accounting Date which were or which should have been known to them at such time and for which provision should have been made in the Final Accounts and for which no provision or to the extent that inadequate provision shall have been made in the Final Accounts

8.3 The [ABC] Partners or (as the case may be) the [123] Partners shall be responsible for and shall jointly and severally indemnify and keep indemnified the New Firm against all claims or potential claims for professional negligence of their respective Firms which had been or should have been notified to the insurers before the Merger Date and for all professional and other costs in connection therewith

8.4 The [ABC] Partners shall be responsible for and shall jointly and severally indemnify and keep indemnified the New Firm against:

[*Set out specific indemnities*]

8.5 The [123] Partners shall be responsible for and shall jointly and severally indemnify and keep indemnified the New Firm against:

[*Set out specific indemnities*]

8.6 As between themselves the [ABC] Partners or (as the case may be) the [123] Partners shall bear the liabilities set out in this Clause in similar manner as if such liabilities had arisen on the Accounting Date

9. TAX ELECTION[3]
    No notice shall be given to H.M. Inspector of Taxes or any other requisite authority and no election shall be made or withdrawn or amended relating to any fiscal matter in connection with the affairs of either of the Parties without the consent of the other in so far as such party may be adversely affected thereby

10. STAFF
    The New Firm shall offer continuation of employment to all members of the staff of the Parties upon at least the same terms as their present employment

11. MUTUAL ASSURANCES
    Each of the Parties undertakes to the other that it has prior to the signing of this Agreement made such disclosure to the other as ought to have been made if the Parties were already Partners

---

[3] This clause is drafted to deal with firms which still have the opportunity to make a continuation election under the old Income and Corporation Taxes Act 1988, s 113 (see Appendix). (These are firms which commenced trade before 6 April 1994 and which have not decided to adopt an actual basis of taxation.) The clause can be deleted for firms which are under the new tax rules for partnerships (the Finance Act 1994, s 215 replacing the Income and Corporation Taxes Act 1988, s 111) at the time of signature of the Agreement and which have no 'open' years on the old basis. Some of the most difficult merger discussions take place over tax elections etc. It is essential that these issues are resolved before the merger takes place.

12.   ANNOUNCEMENTS AND CONFIDENTIALITY

12.1   Neither of the Parties shall make any announcement concerning this Agreement the termination of this Agreement or the negotiations between the Parties unless the form and content of such announcement is agreed by the Parties

12.2   Each of the Parties shall during this Agreement and after its termination use all reasonable endeavours to keep confidential (and to ensure that its employees and agents shall keep confidential) any confidential information relating to or belonging to the other Party and shall not use or disclose such information except with the consent of the other Party

13.   SIGNATURE OF THIS AGREEMENT
        Each of the signatories to this Agreement warrants that he or she is duly authorised by his or her respective firm to enter into this Agreement

SCHEDULE 1
[names of the [ABC] Partners]

SCHEDULE 2
[names of the [123] Partners]

[SCHEDULE 3
[variations to [ABC] Partnership Agreement]]

SIGNED on behalf of [ABC] PARTNERS by	....
SIGNED on behalf of [ABC] PARTNERS by	....
SIGNED on behalf of [123] PARTNERS by	....
SIGNED on behalf of [123] PARTNERS by	....

PRECEDENT 7:   SALARIED PARTNERS AGREEMENT

CONTENTS

PRECEDENT 7: SALARIED PARTNERS AGREEMENT[1]

THIS PARTNERSHIP AGREEMENT[2] executed as a Deed[3] constitutes the terms on which the Partners have agreed to carry on business in partnership[4] as [*trade or profession*] and is intended to be known as[5]

'THE [*name of firm*] 199[. . .] SALARIED PARTNERS AGREEMENT'

1.   DEFINITIONS AND INTERPRETATION

1.1   In this Agreement the following expressions shall where the context so admits have the following meanings

'Equity Partners'   the persons whose names are set out in Part 1 of Schedule X and where the context so admits such of them as shall continue to be Equity Partners in the Firm and any other future Equity Partners for the time being but not any Salaried Partners

'the Firm'   the business presently carried on by the Partners in partnership under the Firm Name

---

[1] This precedent is suitable for a firm which is likely to have a number of salaried partners at the same time. If an Agreement for only one salaried partner is required the following changes would be appropriate.
  1 The Agreement can be dated and the parties set out in the heading.
  2 The actual terms can be set out in Schedule T rather than merely the headings.
  3 There will be minor consequential amendments to other clauses the principal ones of which are noted in notes to the relevant clauses. There are other obvious changes eg from plural to singular.

[2] As drafted, this deed is probably not a Partnership Agreement at all, as the salaried partners do not take part in decision-taking or risk. However, even small changes could change their legal status so an Agreement in this form is desirable.

[3] The Agreement is executed as a deed (Schedule X) to give effect to the following clauses:
  5.1 equity partners indemnity;
  7.3 indemnity as to private debts;
  8.1 trust of property (desirable not essential);
  8.2 property indemnity;
  8.3 removal of property trustee and grant of power of attorney.

[4] This precedent creates an employment for income tax purposes and the salaried partner will be taxed under PAYE. This document is not suitable for so-called Schedule D partners ie partners with no interest in capital and a 'guaranteed' profit share. For further explanation see heading 'Taxation' in 'About the Law' in the Introduction.

[5] As the Agreement may initially be executed by partners on different days, and subsequently executed by new partners, it is identified by a name, and not dated. See 'About the Precedents' in the Introduction and Partnership Act 1890, s 19 (see Appendix) as to variation of partnership deeds.

'Firm Name'	[*X Y and Z*] or any colourable imitation thereof or any combination of names which include any or all of [*X Y or Z*] or any colourable imitation of any such respective names
'Main Agreement'	the separate agreement between the Equity Partners (as varied from time to time)
'Partners'	the Equity Partners [and the Salaried Partners] and where[6] the context so admits such of them as shall continue to be Partners in the Firm and any other future Partners for the time being
'Salaried Partners'	the persons whose names are set out in Part 2 of Schedule X and where the context so admits such of them as shall continue to be Salaried Partners in the Firm and any other future Salaried Partners for the time being
'Terms'[7]	the financial terms and conditions of service of each Salaried Partner including the particulars required by the Trade Union Reform and Employment Rights Act 1993. [The matters to be included in the Terms are set out in Schedule T][8]

1.2   Headings to Clauses and Schedules are for ease of reference only and shall be of no effect in construing the provisions of this Agreement

1.3   Where the context so admits:
   1.3.1   words importing the singular number shall include the plural and words importing the plural number shall include the singular
   1.3.2   references to statutes or to sections of statutes shall include any statutory modifications or re-enactments thereof for the time being in force

2.   DURATION OF PARTNERSHIP
          The partnership by which the Firm is constituted shall continue until terminated in accordance with the Main Agreement

---

[6] If the Agreement is with one salaried partner, this wording will be: 'and the Salaried Partner and any other Salaried Partner . . . '

[7] If the Agreement is with one salaried partner, this clause should be replaced with the following: 'The financial terms and conditions of service of the Salaried Partner are set out in Schedule T which include the particulars required by the Trade Union Reform and Employment Rights Act 1993'.

[8] These words may need to be deleted if the terms are not listed in the deed. See notes 22, 23 below.

3.   EQUITY PARTNERS' RESPONSIBILITY AND AUTHORITY

3.1   The division of profits and losses between the Equity Partners and other matters concerning them as equity partners are contained in the Main Agreement

3.2   All capital requirements of the Firm shall be provided by the Equity Partners to whom the capital and assets of the Firm shall belong

3.3   The Equity Partners shall decide upon:[9]

    3.3.1   the admission and departure of Equity Partners and Salaried Partners

    3.3.2   the merger of the Firm with any other Firm

    3.3.3   the places at which the Firm shall carry on business

    3.3.4   the Firm Name

    3.3.5   the approval of the Firm's accounts

    3.3.6   the meetings of Partners which the Salaried Partners shall be entitled to attend the votes (if any) to which they shall be entitled and the matters upon which they shall be entitled to vote

    3.3.7   the matters reserved to them hereby

    3.3.8   such other matters which they shall decide to reserve to themselves

4.   SALARIED PARTNERS – TERMS AND CONDITIONS OF EMPLOYMENT

[4.1   The Terms relating to each Salaried Partner shall be in accordance with the arrangements made between each Salaried Partner and the Equity Partners from time to time

4.2   In the event of conflict between the Terms and this Agreement the provisions of this Agreement shall prevail][10]

5.   INDEMNITY

The Equity Partners shall meet all the liabilities of the Firm and hereby indemnify each of the Salaried Partners against any claims that may be made against him or her in relation to the liabilities of the Firm except any claim arising from that Salaried Partner's act or default[11]

---

[9]   This is an extensive list of exclusions. It has the effect of making the salaried partners little more than employees. Each firm will have its own approach to their involvement in decision-making and management, and this clause must be considered carefully having regard to the culture of the firm for whom it is being drafted.

[10]   If the Agreement is with one salaried partner, these two clauses should be replaced with the following:

The terms (as amended from time to time) form part of this Agreement'.

[11]   The exception at the end of this clause may give rise to difficulties in negotiation. However, it does not impose an additional liability on the salaried partner. It merely confirms that, if a salaried partner is sued personally for his or her act or default, he or she cannot seek indemnity. If the firm is sued, it could seek indemnity from him or her if the default is negligent. Equally as important, omission of the exception might create problems with the firm's insurers, which might in turn invalidate the firm's negligence insurance.

6.   CHANGES OF SALARIED PARTNERS

6.1   No person shall be admitted as a Salaried Partner otherwise than by a decision of the Equity Partners

6.2   Any person becoming a Salaried Partner shall signify his or her acceptance of this Agreement by signing as a Deed in Part 2 of Schedule X opposite the entry of his or her name

6.3   If any Partner shall cease to be a Partner then the Firm shall not be dissolved as to the other Partners

6.4   There shall be inserted in Part 2 of Schedule X against the entry of the name of any person who has ceased to be a Salaried Partner the date upon which he or she so ceased

7.   GENERAL DUTIES OF THE PARTNERS

7.1   Each Partner shall be just and faithful to the other Partners in all transactions dealings and matters relating to or affecting the Firm and shall in all circumstances give a true and proper account thereof when reasonably required so to do by any of the other Partners [save that no Equity Partner shall be obliged to account to any Salaried Partner in respect of any matter arising under Clause 3.3][12]

7.2   Each Salaried Partner shall devote the whole of his or her time and attention to the business of the Firm and diligently and faithfully employ himself or herself therein and use his or her best endeavours to carry on the same for the utmost benefit of the Firm

7.3   Each Partner shall at all times duly and punctually pay and discharge his or her separate and private debts and engagements whether present or future and keep the property of the Firm and the other Partners and their personal representatives estates and effects indemnified therefrom and from all actions proceedings costs claims and demands in respect thereof

8.   LEASES AND BANKING

8.1   The leases of any premises from time to time used for the purpose of the business and property or securities or other assets of whatsoever kind held by the Firm at the date hereof or hereafter acquired on behalf of the Firm shall be the property of the Firm and shall be held by such of the Partners in whose names the same may from time to time be vested in trust for the Firm

8.2   The Equity Partners hereby indemnify any Salaried Partner or former Salaried Partner in whose name any such property or securities or other assets as aforesaid are for the time being vested (or have previously been vested) against all claims for rent property taxes costs of repairs alterations or improvements and insurance relating to any such property and generally

---

[12]   The exception at the end of this clause confirms that the salaried partner is not in reality a partner in the firm at all. See note 9 above and consider whether to delete the exception.

in respect of any obligations in respect of any such property securities or other assets[13]

8.3   Without prejudice to any statutory power if any Salaried Partner shall cease to be a Partner the Equity Partners may by deed remove him or her from the trusteeship and by the same or any other Deed or Deeds may appoint one or more other persons (whether or not being the person or persons exercising the power) to be a trustee or trustees in place of the Salaried Partner so removed from the trusteeship and may by the same or another deed grant power of attorney to the person or persons so appointed in the name of the Salaried Partner so removed to execute any document necessary to vest the property comprised in the trust in the new trustees thereof[14]

8.4   The Firm shall maintain bank accounts with such bankers as the Equity Partners shall from time to time decide

8.5   All Firm moneys (not required for current expenses) and securities for moneys shall as and when received be paid into or deposited in the Bank to the credit of the Firms accounts. All cheques on such accounts shall be drawn by such mandate as the Equity Partners shall from time to time decide

8.6   No Salaried Partner shall be entitled to open any Firm's bank account without the prior consent of one of the Equity Partners

9.   RESTRICTIONS DURING AGREEMENT
Unless otherwise agreed by the Equity Partners no Salaried Partner shall:

9.1   engage directly or indirectly in any business other than that of the Firm. A Salaried Partner shall be deemed to be engaged in any business (not being a company whose shares are quoted on a recognised stock exchange) inter alia if such Salaried Partner directly or indirectly has an investment in that business or has loaned moneys to that business or entered into guarantees on behalf of that business

9.2   engage or (except for gross misconduct) dismiss any member of the staff of the Firm

9.3   employ any of the money goods or effects of the Firm or pledge the credit thereof [except in the ordinary course of business and upon the account or for the benefit of the Firm][15]

---

[13]   Although such an indemnity is implied, an express indemnity is better. As a result of the recession in the early 1990s, a number of ex-partners have found themselves being sued on leases they signed for their firms many years ago, often without any formal documentation still in existence to prove their indemnity rights. Put a copy of your Partnership Agreement with your will.

[14]   Changes of title to property on partnership changes are often overlooked, and obtaining signatures later can be difficult, expensive and sometimes impossible particularly if a partner has not left on good terms. This clause and the two preceding clauses are all good reasons to execute the Agreement under seal.

[15]   These words should be deleted if salaried partners have no authority to purchase.

9.4   lend money or give credit on behalf of the Firm to or have any dealings
        with any person firm or company whom the Equity Partners have
        previously instructed him or her not to treat or deal with and any loss
        incurred through any breach of this provision shall be made good to the
        Firm by the Salaried Partner incurring the same

9.5   buy order or contract for any goods articles or property on behalf of the
        Firm [in excess of [£1,000] in any one transaction][16] and any goods
        articles or property bought ordered or contracted for by any Salaried
        Partner in breach of this provision shall be taken and paid for by that
        Salaried Partner and shall be his or her separate property unless the Equity
        Partners shall decide to adopt the transaction on behalf of the Firm

9.6   enter into any bond or become bail surety or security with or for any
        person or do or knowingly cause or suffer to be done anything whereby
        the Firm property or any part thereof may be seized attached or taken in
        execution[17]

10.   TERMINATION
10.1   The employment of any Salaried Partner may be terminated by notice in
        accordance with the Terms and such notice shall also be deemed to be
        notice to determine the partnership so far as concerns such Salaried
        Partner on the date specified in the notice in which event such Salaried
        Partner shall cease to be a Salaried Partner and employee on such date

10.2   If any Salaried Partner shall:
        10.2.1 become bankrupt or insolvent or compound or make any
                arrangement with or for the benefit of his or her creditors or
                apply for an interim order pursuant to Section 253 of the
                Insolvency Act 1986 or have a petition for a bankruptcy order
                against him or her presented to the Court
        10.2.2 act in any manner inconsistent with the good faith observable
                between Partners
        10.2.3 be guilty of any conduct which would be a ground for dissolution
                of the Firm by the Court
        10.2.4 absent himself or herself from the Firm without proper cause for
                more than [4] weeks (consecutive or otherwise) in any period of
                12 months[18]
        10.2.5 be convicted of any offence involving fraud or dishonesty or be
                sentenced to a term of imprisonment whether or not sus-
                pended
        10.2.6 be suspended or expelled by the [body]

---

[16] See note 15 above.
[17] Another aspect of the unlimited liability of partners is that the firm is at risk of having its assets
      attacked if a partner does not meet his or her personal obligations. This clause would give grounds
      for dismissal if the firm's assets were attacked by a partner's creditors. Dismissal would not necessarily
      be justified if there was no real risk to the firm.
[18] Even 4 weeks may be too long for unexplained absences.

10.2.7 be guilty of any flagrantly immoral behaviour or of any flagrant deliberate or persistent breach or breaches of the ethics or etiquette of the [. . .] profession or of any other conduct calculated or tending to injure the reputation of the Firm or likely to have a serious or adverse effect upon the Firm's business

10.2.8 commit any substantial breach of this Agreement

then and in any such case the Equity Partners may give notice to determine the partnership so far as concerns such Salaried Partner on the date specified in the notice in which event such Salaried Partner shall cease to be a Salaried Partner and employee on such date

10.3 The Equity Partners may require that the Salaried Partner ceases to be held out as a Salaried Partner during the period following the date of service of notice terminating the partnership and employment of such Salaried Partner

11. SUSPENSION

11.1 Without prejudice to the power of termination conferred by Clause 10 it shall be competent for the Equity Partners to decide without specifying any reason[19] that a Salaried Partner be suspended by being excluded from attending to the business and affairs of the Firm from such date and for such period as they may specify not exceeding in the first instance 6 weeks

11.2 From the date specified the Partner concerned shall forthwith absent himself or herself from the Firm's premises and thereafter take no part in the business or affairs of the Firm or its clients for the period of suspension. Such suspension may be extended from time to time by further decisions as aforesaid. Insofar as he or she may otherwise be entitled to attend or vote at meetings of Partners a Partner who has been suspended shall not be so entitled during a period of suspension

11.3 During any period of suspension the Partner concerned shall continue to be entitled to his or her salary and other rights of a Partner except as set out in Clause 11.2

12. RESTRICTIONS FOLLOWING TERMINATION[20]

12.1 From the date that he or she ceases to be a Salaried Partner a Salaried Partner shall not:

12.1.1 at any time thereafter solicit whether by himself or herself or as a partner or employee of any other person firm or company any person firm or company who shall have been a client of the Firm (other than his or her relatives or a company wholly owned or

---

[19] It is inappropriate to specify a reason as this clause will normally be used when a dismissal is in contemplation, to allow for investigation.

[20] These restrictions are by way of guidance only. Careful consideration must be given in each case having regard to the size of the firm, its business, its location and the other factors taken into account when considering the enforceability of restrictive covenants in *employment* contracts.

controlled by him or her or his or her relatives) at any time during a period of 3 years immediately preceding the date when he or she ceased to be a Partner

12.1.2   for a period of 3 years thereafter act as a [*occupation*] for any such client in manner aforesaid

12.1.3   during a period of 3 years thereafter carry on or be concerned or engaged or interested whether directly or indirectly and whether by himself or herself or as a partner or employee of any other person firm or company in the [practice or profession of *or* business of . . .] within a radius of [one mile] from any address at which at the date of his or her ceasing to be a partner the Firm shall be carrying on the Firm practice

12.1.4   at any time thereafter and in any place practise under any style or name which shall include or refer to the Firm Name

12.1.5   at any time suggest or cause to be suggested to any member of the Firm's staff that he or she might leave the employment of the Firm to work for the Salaried Partner or for any company or firm with which the Salaried Partner is or intends to be connected

12.1.6   at any time encourage or cause to be encouraged any such staff as aforesaid to leave the employment of the Firm to work as aforesaid

12.2   It is hereby declared that the provisions of each of the respective sub-clauses of Clause 12.1 are intended to be read and construed independently of each other so that none of such separate provisions (or any of the other provisions of this Agreement) shall be dependent on any one or more of any of the other such provisions

13   VARIATION OF THIS AGREEMENT
13.1   This Agreement may be varied by the Equity Partners such variation to take effect in respect of each Salaried Partner upon notification of the variation to him or her in writing

13.2   No such variation shall take effect so as to adversely affect any Salaried Partner's Terms or his or her rights or impose greater obligations under Clauses 3, 5 or 12 of this Agreement

14.   GENERAL
14.1   Save as herein otherwise provided all disputes and questions whatsoever which shall either during the partnership or afterwards arise between the Partners or their respective representatives or between any Partners or Partner and the representatives of any other Partners touching these presents or the construction or application thereof or as to any act deed or omission of any Partner or as to any other matter in any way relating to the Firm business or the affairs thereof or the rights duties or liabilities of any person under this Agreement shall be referred to a single arbitrator who shall be appointed by the Partners involved in the dispute if they can agree upon one or (failing agreement) by the President for the time being of the

[*body*] on the application of any Partner and in either case in accordance with and subject to the provisions of the Arbitration Acts 1950 to 1979[21]

14.2   Any notice authorised or required to be given or served by this Agreement shall be deemed to be duly served if the same shall be delivered personally to the person to whom it is intended to be given or shall be sent by post in a pre-paid letter sent by recorded delivery or by registered post and addressed to him or her either at his or her last known place of abode in England or (if it is reasonable to expect that he or she will receive it within 72 hours) left for him or her in the room of the Partnership premises in which he or she habitually worked as a Partner and where so sent or left shall be deemed to be served on the first working day of the Firm which shall follow the day on which such letter would in the ordinary course of post have been delivered or the day on which the same shall have been left

14.3   A notice to the Equity Partners shall be properly served if delivered to or served upon any Equity Partner in accordance with this Clause

---

[21]   Partnership disputes before the courts should be avoided. Arbitration is the most suitable procedure for partners. Some firms name the arbitrator in their Agreement, often their solicitor. However, some firms may not wish to give a salaried partner the right to go to arbitration.

SCHEDULE T[22]

[Matters to be Included in the Terms][23]

1. Date of commencement of employment and whether previous employment is continuous
2. Job title
3. Normal working hours
4. Place of work and confirmation that the Salaried Partner is not expected to work outside the UK
5. Confirmation that the employment is expected to be permanent
6. Confirmation that no collective agreements directly affect the terms and conditions of the employment
7. Salary and payment intervals
8. Bonus/Commission
9. Benefits
10. Car
11. Holiday entitlement (including public holidays) holiday pay and entitlement to accrued holiday pay on termination of the employment
12. Maternity leave
13. Sick leave
14. Pension and whether a contracting-out certificate is in force
15. Notice period
16. Grievance and disciplinary procedures

[22] This Schedule is only intended to set out the *headings* which will go in a separate memorandum if the Agreement is with more than one salaried partner. The headings should follow the general form of the firm's staff contracts. This keeps confidentiality of earnings between salaried partners. As the Schedule is only an aide memoire it could be omitted.

[23] If the Agreement is with one salaried partner, this heading should be 'The Terms'. The Schedule will then set out the actual terms of employment.

SCHEDULE X

Details of Partners and Execution

[This Deed is intended to be delivered by each Partner on the date of delivery opposite that Partner's name

or

[. . .] is duly authorised to execute this Deed on behalf of the Equity Partners. This Deed is intended to be delivered by the Equity Partners on the date of delivery opposite the name of [. . .] and by each Salaried Partner on the date of delivery opposite that Partner's name][24]

Part 1
Equity Partners

Name and address	Signature as a Deed	Date of Delivery	Signature of Witness
[name (1)]	....		....
[name (2)]	....		....
[name (3)]	....		....
[name (4)]	....		....

---

[24] Alternative introductory wording is given. Some Partnership Agreements contain power of attorney for one partner to execute deeds on behalf of the firm. See Precedent 1: Standard Partnership Agreement, Clause 11.1 at p 31. Failing this, either all equity partners must sign, or the document should be under hand only. See note 3 above. Part 1 of the Schedule will need amendment to list only the names (apart from the signing partner) but not the signatures, of the equity partners.

Part 2
Salaried Partners

Name and address	Signature as a Deed	Dates	Signature of Witness
[name (1)]	....	Date of delivery .... Date ceasing	....
[name (2)]	....	Date of delivery .... Date ceasing	....
[name (3)]	....	Date of delivery .... Date ceasing	....
[name (4)]	....	Date of delivery .... Date ceasing	....

PRECEDENT 8: ADMISSION DEED FOR NEW PARTNER

CONTENTS

PRECEDENT 8: ADMISSION DEED FOR NEW PARTNER[1]

THIS ADMISSION DEED[2] dated the [. . .] day of [. . .] 199[. . .] BETWEEN

(1) THE PARTNERS

(2) THE NEW PARTNER

executed as a Deed[3] constitutes the terms upon which the New Partner is admitted as a Partner in the Firm of [*name of firm*]

1.	DEFINITIONS AND INTERPRETATION	
1.1	In this Deed the following expressions shall where the context so admits have the following meanings[4]	

'Accounting Date'	the date up to which the Annual Accounts are drawn
'Accounting Period'	the period from one Accounting Date to the next Accounting Date
'Admission Date'	[*date*]
'Agreement'	The [[*name of firm*] 199[. . .] Partnership Agreement *or other description of the Partnership Agreement*] whereby the Parties have carried on business as [*trade or profession*] under the Firm Name
'Annual Accounts'	the accounts drawn in accordance with the Agreement
'Firm'	the business hitherto carried on by the Partners in partnership under the Firm Name pursuant to the Agreement and to be carried on by the Parties

---

[1] This precedent is only a guideline document, as any admission of a new partner which is not directly in accordance with the Partnership Agreement will, of necessity, be a unique document. An Admission Deed is not necessary if the Partnership Agreement contains appropriate admission provisions unless those provisions are being varied, or those provisions are unclear (perhaps because there is no written agreement).

[2] With the widespread use of word processing it has become easier to re-execute documents in their amended form rather than have numerous deeds of variation, retirement and admission. Consideration could therefore be given to a new Agreement rather than this Deed.

[3] Executed as a deed because of the indemnity contained in Clause 4.2. Otherwise a deed is not essential, even if the original Agreement is under seal, by virtue of the Partnership Act 1890, s 19 (see Appendix).

[4] Not all of these definitions may be necessary, depending on the words defined in the Partnership Agreement of the firm for whom this Deed is prepared.

'Firm Name'	[*X Y and Z*] or any colourable imitation thereof or any combination of names which include any or all of [*X Y or Z*] or any colourable imitation of any such respective names
'New Partner'	The person whose name is set out in Part 2 of Schedule X
'Parties'	the parties to this Deed
'Partners'	the persons whose names are set out in Part 1 of Schedule X
'the Partnership'	the partnership hitherto subsisting between the Partners and being continued by the Parties including any partnership which is a successor to that partnership under whatever name

1.2   Headings to Clauses and Schedules are for ease of reference only and shall be of no effect in construing the provisions of this Agreement

1.3   Where the context so admits:

    1.3.1   words importing the singular number shall include the plural and words importing the plural number shall include the singular

    1.3.2   references to statutes or to sections of statutes shall include any statutory modifications or re-enactments thereof for the time being in force

    1.3.3   [words defined in the Agreement shall where the context so admits have the same meaning in this Deed][5]

2.   ADMISSION

2.1   The New Partner [was *or* will be] admitted as a Partner in the Partnership on the Admission Date

3.   FINANCIAL

3.1   The New Partner shall contribute the sum of [£ . . .] to the capital of the Partnership [on the signing of this Deed *or* by the following instalments] [*set out payment arrangements including interest if appropriate*]

3.2   Capital contributions profits shares and drawings of the Parties with effect from the Admission Date shall be as set out in Schedule F

[3.3   Annual Accounts shall not be prepared at the Admission Date but instead the profit share of the New Partner for the current Accounting Period shall be the percentage set out in column 3 of Schedule F of the profits of the Firm for the current Accounting Period][6]

---

[5]   This subclause will not be necessary if no definitions from the Partnership Agreement are used. If possible the same definitions should be used in both documents to avoid confusion.

[6]   This clause will not be necessary if the new partner is admitted on an accounting date.

4.   TAXATION[7]

4.1   Upon or after the admission of the New Partner all Partners (including the
            New Partner) shall if so Resolved by the Partners join in giving to H.M.
            Inspector of Taxes or any other requisite authority in such form as may be
            required any notice and join in making any election or the withdrawal or
            amendment thereof relating to any fiscal matter in connection with the
            affairs of the Partnership and for this purpose shall sign any such document
            and do any such act and provide any such information as shall be necessary
            to give effect to such Resolution[8]

[4.2   The Partners (other than the New Partner) shall indemnify the New
            Partner from and against any taxation of whatsoever nature suffered in
            excess of what would have been suffered by the New Partner as a result of
            [his *or* her] admission as a Partner had such notice or election or
            withdrawal or amendment thereof (as the case may be) not been given][9]

5.   VARIATION OF THE AGREEMENT

5.1   The Agreement shall be varied as set out in Schedule V

5.2   The Agreement shall have effect from the Admission Date as varied by this
            Deed

---

[7] This clause will not be necessary if the parties are to be subject to individual assessment under the
     provisions of the Income and Corporation Taxes Act 1988, s 111 (as substituted by the Finance Act
     1994, s 215) (see Appendix).
[8] The defined terms 'Resolved' and 'Resolution' in this clause may need to be amended to accord with
     the decision-taking rules of the firm.
[9] Many firms do not consider it appropriate to give this indemnity to a new partner.

SCHEDULE F

Capital Contributions Profit Shares and Drawings

Capital contributions profits shares and drawings with effect from the Admission Date shall be as follows:

Partner	Capital	Profit share Accounting Period ending [date][10]	Profit share Accounting Periods after [date]	Monthly drawings
[name (1)]	£	[. . .]%	[. . .]%	£
[name (2)]	£	[. . .]%	[. . .]%	£
[name (3)]	£	[. . .]%	[. . .]%	£
[name (4)]	£	[. . .]%	[. . .]%	£
New Partner	*£	[. . .]%	[. . .]%	£
Total	£	100%	100%	£

* The New Partner's capital is payable as set out in Clause 3.1

---

[10] This column will not be necessary if the new partner is admitted on an accounting date. See Clause 3.3.

SCHEDULE V

Variations of the Agreement

[*Here set out variations to the Partnership Agreement. These may be specific to the New Partner – for example the New Partner's holiday entitlement, outside business interests, pension contributions or restrictive covenants. The opportunity may also be taken to introduce new provisions of more general application – for example drawings limits or maternity leave.*]

SCHEDULE X

Details of Partners and Execution

This Deed is intended to be delivered on the date hereof
[[. . .] is duly authorised to execute this Deed on behalf of the Partners][11]

Part 1
Partners

Name and Address	Signature as a Deed	Signature of Witness
[name (1)]	....	....
[name (2)]	....	....
[name (3)]	....	....
[name (4)]	....	....

Part 2
The New Partner

Name and Address	Signature as a Deed	Signature of Witness
[name]	....	....

[11] Some Partnership Agreements contain power of attorney for one partner to execute deeds on behalf of the firm. See Precedent 1: Standard Partnership Agreement, Clause 11.1 at p 31. Failing this, all partners must sign. Part 1 of the Schedule will need amendment to list only the names (apart from the signing partner) but not the signatures, of the equity partners.

PRECEDENT 9:   RETIREMENT DEED FOR EXISTING PARTNER

CONTENTS

PRECEDENT 9: RETIREMENT DEED FOR EXISTING PARTNER[1]

THIS RETIREMENT DEED dated the [. . .] day of [. . .] 199[. . .] BETWEEN

(1) THE PARTNERS

(2) THE RETIRING PARTNER

executed as a Deed[2] constitutes the terms upon which the Retiring Partner retires as a Partner in the Firm of [name of firm]

1.	DEFINITIONS AND INTERPRETATION	
1.1	In this Deed the following expressions shall where the context so admits have the following meanings[3]	

'Accounting Date'	the date up to which the Annual Accounts are drawn
'Accounting Period'	the period from one Accounting Date to the next Accounting Date
'Advance'	[the amount advanced to the Firm by the Retiring Partner][£ . . .]
'Agreement'	[The [name of firm] 199[. . .] Partnership Agreement or other description of the Partnership Agreement] whereby the Parties have carried on business as [trade or profession] under the Firm Name
'Annual Accounts'	the accounts drawn in accordance with the Agreement
'Capital Account'	the share of the Retiring Partner in the capital of the Partnership
'Firm'	the business hitherto carried on by the Parties in partnership under the Firm Name pursuant to the Agreement and to be carried on by the Partners
'Firm Name'	[X Y and Z] or any colourable imitation thereof or any combination of names

---

[1] This precedent is only a guideline document, as any retirement which is not directly in accordance with the Partnership Agreement will, of necessity, be a unique document. A Retirement Deed is not necessary if the Partnership Agreement contains appropriate retirement provisions unless those provisions are being varied, or those provisions are unclear (perhaps because there is no written agreement).

[2] Executed as a deed because of Clauses 5.2, 6.2, and 7.

[3] Not all of these definitions may be necessary, depending on the words defined in the Partnership Agreement of the firm for whom this Deed is prepared.

which include any or all of [*X Y or Z*] or
any colourable imitation of any such
respective names

'Parties'   the parties to this Deed

'Partners'   the persons whose names are set out in
                             Part 1 of Schedule X and where the
                             context so admits such of them as shall
                             continue to be Partners in the Partner-
                             ship and any other future Partners for
                             the time being

'the Partnership'   the partnership hitherto subsisting
                             between the Parties and being continued
                             by the Partners including any partner-
                             ship which is a successor to that partner-
                             ship under whatever name

'Partnership Accountants'   Messrs [. . .]

['Retirement Accounts'[4]   Annual Accounts of the Partnership to
                             be prepared on a consistent basis with
                             the previous 3 years Annual Accounts
                             [and approved by the Parties][5] within [3]
                             months after the Retirement Date [but
                             with the following variations [. . .][6]]]

'Retirement Capital'[7]   [the amount shown as due to the Retir-
                             ing Partner in the Retirement
                             Accounts]

                             or

                             [a sum equal to the amount of capital
                             standing to the credit of the Retiring
                             Partner in [his *or* her] Capital Account
                             on the Retirement Date after adding [his
                             or her] profit share (after actual drawings)
                             from the previous Accounting Date
                             until the Retirement Date]

                             and after deducting therefrom[8]

                             1. such sum as [in the opinion of the
                                Partnership Accountants] may be re-
                                quired to satisfy [his *or* her] share of

---

4 Include this clause if retirement accounts are to be prepared.

5 Include if the retiring partner is to approve the retirement accounts.

6 There are numerous variations to retirement accounts the most common of which are a revised basis
   of valuation of (1) work in progress; (2) vehicles computers and other fixed assets; and (3)
   property.

7 Depending on whether or not retirement accounts are to be drawn.

8 For firms which are on the new tax rules for partnerships under the Finance Act 1994, s 215
   (replacing the Income and Corporation Taxes Act 1988, s 111) (see Appendix) at the time of
   signature of the Deed and which have no 'open' years on the old basis, the words in brackets can be
   deleted. See note 17 below.

	any income tax assessment which may be made upon the Partnership for any year of assessment ended prior to the Retirement Date; and

2. the appropriate proportion of [his *or* her] share of any income tax assessment for the year of assessment in which the Retirement Date falls]

'Retirement Date'	[*date*]
'Retirement Interest'	interest at [... per cent per annum above the base rate of [...] Bank plc from time to time] computed with [6 monthly] rests[9]
'Retiring Partner'	The person whose name is set out in Part 2 of Schedule X
'Retiring Partner's Clients'	those clients of the Partnership at the Retirement Date set out in Schedule C

1.2   Headings to Clauses and Schedules are for ease of reference only and shall be of no effect in construing the provisions of this Agreement

1.3   Where the context so admits:

    1.3.1   words importing the singular number shall include the plural and words importing the plural number shall include the singular

    1.3.2   references to statutes or to sections of statutes shall include any statutory modifications or re-enactments thereof for the time being in force

    1.3.3   [words defined in the Agreement shall where the context so admits have the same meaning in this Deed][10]

2.   VARIATION OF THE AGREEMENT

[All provisions affecting the retirement of the Retiring Partner] *or* [Clauses [...], [...], and [...]] in the Agreement shall cease to have effect and in lieu thereof the provisions of this Deed shall apply and subject thereto the Retiring Partner shall have no rights whatsoever against any Partner

3.   RETIREMENT

3.1   The Retiring Partner [retired *or* will retire] from the Partnership on the Retirement Date [by reason of [...]][11]

---

9   The interest rate could be the same as the rate at which the firm borrows funds from its bankers. There is no reason for the firm to profit from the capital of a retired partner, although its retention will help cash flow.

10   This subclause will not be necessary if no definitions from the Partnership Agreement are used. If possible the same definitions should be used in both documents to avoid confusion.

11   Here set out reasons for retirement if it is desired to record them, or if continuing provisions in the Agreement are relevant to the reason for departure.

3.2   The retirement of the Retiring Partner from the Partnership shall not dissolve the partnership as between the Partners[12]

4.   FINANCIAL

4.1   On the Retirement Date the profit share of the Retiring Partner shall be cancelled and the Partners shall succeed to all the interest of the Retiring Partner in the Partnership (subject to [his *or* her] rights herein contained) [and the Partners shall share profits from the Retirement Date in the shares set against their names in Schedule X][13]

4.2   Amounts due to the Retiring Partner shall be repaid as follows:[14]

    4.2.1   any Advance made by [him *or* her] together with all accrued interest at the Retirement Date shall be repaid to [him *or* her] or [his *or* her] personal representatives within [3] months after [his *or* her] Retirement Date

    4.2.2   [any tax reserve[15] held for [him *or* her] together with all accrued interest at [his *or* her] Termination Date shall be repaid to [him *or* her] or [his *or* her] personal representatives within [3] months after [his *or* her] Retirement Date]

    4.2.3   the Retirement Capital of the Retiring Partner shall be repaid to [him *or* her] by [6] equal [6-monthly] instalments the first of such instalments to be paid to [him *or* her] [6] months after [his *or* her] Retirement Date

    4.2.4   Retirement Interest calculated from the Retirement Date shall be paid with each payment of [his *or* her] Advance (including accrued interest to [his *or* her] Retirement Date) and [his *or* her] Retirement Capital

4.3   If and so far as it shall be necessary to apportion profits and losses for any period the apportionment shall be on a time basis by reference to the then current Accounting Period

4.4   Sums retained from Retirement Capital for income tax which are not required to satisfy the Retiring Partner's share of any income tax assessments which may be made upon the Partnership shall be credited to the Retirement Capital of the Retiring Partner (or paid to [him *or* her] if [his *or* her] Retirement Capital has been repaid) as soon as the relevant

---

[12]   This will not be necessary if this clause is in the Agreement.

[13]   Remaining partners may prefer to put their future arrangements in a separate document.

[14]   Payments on retirement can consist of five elements:
   1   repayment of advances;
   2   repayment of tax reserve;
   3   profit share from the last accounting date to the retirement date;
   4   retirement capital;
   5   retirement interest.
   These may be paid by the same or different instalments. This precedent assumes that items 1 and 2, and 3 and 4 are paid together. If not, the definition of retirement capital may need to be changed as well as this clause.

[15]   See Precedent 1: Standard Partnership Agreement, Clause F8.1 at p 38.

income tax assessment has been agreed with the Inland Revenue and any deficiency in any sum so retained shall be reimbursed by the Retiring Partner on demand

4.5   If at the date that payment of any instalment of Retirement Capital or Retirement Interest is due the amount of such payment has not been ascertained then a reasonable amount on account of such payment shall be made on such date and the remainder of such payment shall be made as soon as the same shall have been ascertained

5.   TRANSFER OF ASSETS AND PROPERTY
5.1   The Parties shall as soon as possible and subject to obtaining any necessary consents use their best reasonable efforts (without incurring expenditure other than upon professional fees) to transfer the legal ownership of the assets and property listed in Schedule A (which are beneficially owned by the Partnership from the Retirement Date) to the Partners and to obtain a release of the Retiring Partner from liability including liability to the Firm's bankers[16]

5.2   The Partners hereby indemnify the Retiring Partner against all claims for rent property taxes costs of repairs alterations or improvements and insurance relating to any such property and generally in respect of any obligations in respect of any such assets or other property

6.   TAXATION[17]
6.1   The Parties shall join in giving to H.M. Inspector of Taxes or any other requisite authority in such form as may be required any notice and join in making any election or the withdrawal or amendment thereof relating to any fiscal matter in connection with the affairs of the Partnership as may be decided by the Partners and for this purpose shall sign any such document and do any such act and provide any such information as shall be necessary to give effect to such decision

6.2   The Partners hereby indemnify the Retiring Partner from and against any taxation of whatsoever nature suffered by [him *or* her] or [his *or* her] estate as a result of ceasing to be a Partner in excess of what would have been suffered by the Retiring Partner had such notice or election or withdrawal or amendment thereof (as the case may be) not been given

7.   GENERAL INDEMNITY
        In addition to the liabilities and obligations undertaken pursuant to this Deed the Partners shall undertake all the debts liabilities and obligations of

[16]   Normally, a new bank mandate is signed at retirement which releases the retiring partner. If not the bank may freeze the accounts. In view of the difficulties of obtaining a release from a landlord, it may be preferable to exclude leases from the obligation to obtain a release.

[17]   This clause may not be necessary unless there are still 'open' years of assessment of the firm (as opposed to individual partners) under the provisions of the Income and Corporation Taxes Act 1988, s 111 (as substituted by the Finance Act 1994, s 215) (see Appendix).

the Retiring Partner from the Retirement Date other than such as are hereby deemed to be for [his *or* her] separate account or are directly or indirectly attributable to any act or omission of the Retiring Partner but without prejudice to any subsisting liability of the Retiring Partner for breach of the Agreement and will indemnify and keep the Retiring Partner indemnified against all such debts liabilities and obligations[18]

8.   RESTRICTIONS[19]
The Retiring Partner shall not:

8.1   at any time solicit whether by [himself *or* herself] or as a partner or employee of any other person firm or company directly or indirectly any person firm or company who shall have been a client of the Firm [other than the Retiring Partner's Clients[20]] at any time during a period of 3 years immediately preceding the Retirement Date

8.2   for a period of 3 years from the date of ceasing to be a Partner act as a [*occupation*] for any such client in manner aforesaid

8.3   during a period of 3 years from the Retirement Date carry on or be concerned or engaged or interested whether directly or indirectly and whether by [himself *or* herself] or as a partner or employee of any other person firm or company in the [practice or profession of *or* business of . . .] within a radius of [one mile] from any address at which at the Retirement Date the Partnership shall be carrying on the Partnership practice[21]

8.4   at any time after the Retirement Date and in any place practise under any style or name which shall include or refer to the Firm Name

8.5   at any time suggest or cause to be suggested to any member of the Firm's staff that he or she might leave the employment of the Firm to work for the Retiring Partner or for any company or firm with which the Retiring Partner is or intends to be connected

---

[18] This clause can give rise to many difficulties.
          First, it must be made clear that a partner will not be indemnified against his own default. So a partner who is expelled for cause remains liable to indemnify his former partners against loss arising from that default. A Retirement Deed is unusual in the case of expulsion.
          Second, a partner who is negligent remains liable to indemnify for his or her own negligence. This is not an issue if the firm has sufficient negligence insurance to cover a claim, as the insurance extends to all partners, including one who is negligent. Moreover, in most cases of negligence, the claim rarely arises exclusively from one person's mistake, making claims difficult to pursue inside a firm.
          Third is the liability of all partners for negligence claims in excess of the firm's insurance cover. My view is that, if such a claim has been intimated at the retirement date, a reserve should be included in the retirement accounts but, if not, the retiring partner should get a full indemnity against future claims, whenever the negligent act happened.

[19] These restrictions are by way of guidance only. Careful consideration must be given in each case having regard to the size of the firm, its business, its location and the other factors taken into account when considering the enforceability of restrictive covenants.

[20] If the retiring partner is permitted to take clients then suitable provisions should be inserted as to (1) payment for work in progress and (2) access to papers by the partners.

[21] It may be preferable to list the premises.

8.6   at any time encourage or cause to be encouraged any such staff as aforesaid to leave the employment of the Firm to work as aforesaid

It is hereby declared that the provisions of each of Clauses 8.1 to 8.6 respectively are intended to be read and construed independently of each other so that none of such separate provisions shall be dependent on any one or more of any of the other such provisions

9.   GENERAL
9.1   This Deed constitutes the whole of the agreement between the Parties

9.2   All disputes and questions whatsoever which shall arise between the Parties touching these presents or the construction or application thereof or any account valuation or division of assets debts or liabilities to be made hereunder or the rights duties or liabilities of any person under this Agreement shall be referred to a single arbitrator who shall be appointed by the Parties involved in the dispute if they can agree upon one or (failing agreement) by the [President for the time being of the [*body*]] on the application of any Party and in either case in accordance with and subject to the provisions of the Arbitration Acts 1950 to 1979[22]

9.3   Any notice authorised or required to be given or served by this Deed shall be deemed to be duly served if the same shall be delivered personally to the person to whom it is intended to be given or shall be sent by post in a pre-paid letter sent by recorded delivery or by registered post and addressed to him or her either at his or her last known place of abode in England and where so sent or left shall be deemed to be served on the first working day of the Firm which shall follow the day on which such letter would in the ordinary course of post have been delivered or the day on which the same shall have been left

9.4   If any of the Parties so requires due notice of the fact of the Retiring Partner leaving the Partnership shall be given by advertisement in the London Gazette and by notice in writing to the Commissioners of H.M. Customs & Excise[23] and each of the Parties shall sign and concur in all necessary or proper notices for that purpose

9.5   Each of the Parties agrees that he or she will execute and do all such deeds documents and things as may be necessary to carry this Deed into effect

---

[22]   Partnership disputes before the courts should be avoided. Arbitration is a most suitable procedure for partners. Some firms name the arbitrator, often their solicitor.

[23]   Value Added Tax Act 1994, s 45(2) treats a retiring partner as continuing to be a partner for VAT purposes until the partnership change is notified to Customs & Excise.

SCHEDULE A

Property and Other Assets

[list property and assets]

SCHEDULE C

Clients for Whom the Retiring Partner May Act

1   The relatives of the Retiring Partner and companies wholly owned or
           controlled by the Retiring Partner or [his *or* her] relatives

[2   *[other clients]*]]

SCHEDULE X

Details of Partners, Partners' New Profit Shares, the Retiring Partner and Execution

This Deed is intended to be delivered on the date of this Deed
[[. . .] is duly authorised to execute this Deed on behalf of the Partners][24]

Part 1
Partners

Name and Address	New profit share[25]	Signature as a Deed	Signature of Witness
[name (1)]	[. . .]%	....	....
[name (2)]	[. . .]%	....	....
[name (3)]	[. . .]%	....	....
[name (4)]	[. . .]%	....	....

Part 2
The Retiring Partner

Name and Address	Signature as a Deed	Signature of Witness
[name]	....	....

[24] Some Partnership Agreements contain power of attorney for one partner to execute deeds on behalf of the firm. See Precedent 1: Standard Partnership Agreement, Clause 11.1 at p 31. In this case, Part 1 of the Schedule will need amendment to list only the names (apart from the signing partner) but not the signatures, of the partners.

[25] See note 13 above as to profit shares.

PRECEDENT 10:   NOTICE OF RETIREMENT[1]

[*X Y and Z*]
[*address*]
[*date*]

We wish to notify you that [*name*] [retired as *or* ceased to be] a Partner in this firm on [*date*]. All debts due to or from the firm will be received and paid by the remaining partners who continue the business and whose names are printed on this letter.

....
[signed]
Partner

---

[1] No particular formality is required for this notice which is issued to protect the departing partner against liability for debts incurred after the date of retirement, and to protect the remaining partners against actions taken by the departing partner who might otherwise continue to be held out as a partner in the firm.

Quite apart from this there will no doubt be good public relations reasons for writing to clients on the departure of a partner. If there is only a wish to give notice for legal reasons, a notice in the *London Gazette* and to Customs & Excise in respect of VAT will be sufficient.

PRECEDENT 11: RESOLUTION TO TERMINATE AND/OR SUSPEND[1]

[name of firm]

Minutes of a meeting of the Partners duly convened in accordance with Clause M1 of the [name of firm] 199[. . .] Partnership Agreement and held at [address] on [date]

Present
[in person]
[list names]

[by proxy]
[list names] represented by [name of proxies][2]

RETIREMENT DUE TO INCAPACITY[3]
[It was reported to the meeting that [name of Partner] had been incapacitated from performing [his or her] duties as a Partner for a total of at least [125 working days] in the period commencing [date] and ending [date].
or
It was reported to the meeting Dr [name] had expressed the view that [name of Partner] was likely to be incapacitated from performing [his or her] duties as a Partner for a total of at least [125 working days] in the period commencing [date] and ending [date].]

It was accordingly unanimously RESOLVED by the Partners eligible to vote on this Resolution that [name of Partner] shall retire from the Partnership on [date] and shall cease to be a Partner on such date.

EXPULSION[4]
It was reported to the meeting that [name of Partner] had [here list one or more of the grounds for expulsion set out in the Agreement eg 'acted in a manner inconsistent with the good faith observable between Partners in that he had paid into his private bank account cash received for fees due to the Firm and subsequently authorised the debt to be written off in the Firm's books as a bad debt']

It was accordingly unanimously RESOLVED by the Partners eligible to vote on this Resolution that the Partnership shall be determined so far as it concerns

---

[1] These resolutions are all based on Precedent 1: 'Standard Partnership Agreement'. That precedent does not require service of notice on the partner leaving or suspended (although it would be polite to tell him or her if he or she does not attend the meeting!). A form of notice is included as Precedent 12: Notice of Termination or Suspension. In adapting these drafts it is good practice to follow the wording of the relevant clause in the Agreement.

[2] Omit if the Agreement does not contain provisions for proxy voting.

[3] See Precedent 1: Standard Partnership Agreement, Clause T6 at p 58.

[4] See Precedent 1: Standard Partnership Agreement, Clause T7 at p 59.

[*name of Partner*] on [*date*] and that [he *or* she] shall cease to be a Partner on such date. [It was further RESOLVED by the Partners eligible to vote on this Resolution that [*name of Partner*] be forthwith suspended by being excluded from attending to the business and affairs of the Partnership until such date.]

COMPULSORY RETIREMENT[5]

A copy of the proposed resolution having been given to all Partners at least 28 days before the meeting it was unanimously RESOLVED by the Partners eligible to vote on this Resolution that [*name of Partner*] shall be compelled to retire from the Partnership on [*date*][6] and shall cease to be a Partner on such date. [It was further RESOLVED by the Partners eligible to vote on this Resolution that [*name of Partner*] be forthwith suspended by being excluded from attending to the business and affairs of the Partnership until such date.]

SUSPENSION[7]

It was unanimously RESOLVED by the Partners eligible to vote on this Resolution that [*name of Partner*] be suspended by being excluded from attending to the business and affairs of the Partnership from [*date*] until [*date*].

---

[5]   See Precedent 1: Standard Partnership Agreement, Clause T8 at p 60.

[6]   Note that under Precedent 1: Standard Partnership Agreement, Clause R5.3 a partner subject to compulsory retirement may be entitled to an additional profit share. This may affect the decision as to retirement date.

[7]   See Precedent 1: Standard Partnership Agreement, Clause T9 at p 60.

PRECEDENT 12: NOTICE OF TERMINATION AND/OR SUSPENSION[1]

[name of firm]

To [*Name of Partner*][2]

At a meeting of the Partners duly convened in accordance with Clause [. . .] of the [*name of firm*] 199[. . .] Partnership Agreement and held at [*address*] on [*date*] the following Resolution was passed:

[*quote resolution verbatim*]

[We therefore give you notice [expelling][3] you from the Partnership on [*date*]

or

We therefore give you notice suspending you by excluding you from attending to the business and affairs of the Partnership from [*date*] for a period of [. . . *days*] (expiring on [*date*])]

Dated   199[. . .]

Signed ....[4]

---

[1] This notice gives a general indication of format. The notice must comply with the terms of the Agreement. The precedents in this book do not require service of notice on a partner leaving or suspended.

[2] To be addressed and served in accordance with the provisions of the Agreement.

[3] Or as appropriate according to the resolution.

[4] This may need to be signed by all partners depending on the terms of the Agreement. Consideration should be given to including authority for one partner to sign when passing the resolution.

PRECEDENT 13:   TRUST DEED FOR PARTNERSHIP PROPERTY

CONTENTS

PRECEDENT 13:   TRUST DEED FOR PARTNERSHIP PROPERTY[1]

THIS TRUST DEED[2] dated the [. . .] day of [. . .] 199[. . .] BETWEEN

(1)   THE TRUSTEES

(2)   THE PARTNERS[3]

executed as a Deed constitutes the terms upon which the Trustees hold the Property for the Partners

1.	DEFINITIONS AND INTERPRETATION
1.1	In this Deed the following expressions shall where the context so admits have the following meanings[4]

'Agreement'	[The [*name of firm*] 199[. . .] Partnership Agreement *or other description of the Partnership Agreement*] whereby the Partners carry on business as [*trade or profession*] under the Firm Name
'Firm'	the business carried on by the Partners in partnership under the Firm Name pursuant to the Agreement
'Firm Name'	[*X Y and Z*] or any colourable imitation thereof or any combination of names which include any or all of [*X Y or Z*] or any colourable imitation of any such respective names
'Partners'	the persons whose names are set out in Part 1 of Schedule X and where the context so admits such of them as shall continue to be Partners in the Firm and

---

[1] A single form of deed is used for both freehold and leasehold properties. Such a deed is not necessary if the Partnership Agreement contains Clauses 5.2 to 5.4 in Precedent 1: Standard Partnership Agreement.

[2] It is preferable to keep Declarations of Trust in separate documents rather than in the Transfer or Lease – off the title. This is particularly the case with registered land where the Land Registry keep the original transfer. If it is preferred to insert wording in the lease, appropriate wording is given in Precedent 15: Trust Clauses. Ideally, land should be vested in two companies as trustees and agents for the firm. Such documentation is outside the scope of this book.

[3] It will not be necessary for the partners to join in if there is already an indemnity like that contained in Clause 5.3 in Precedent 1: Standard Partnership Agreement in the Partnership Agreement of the firm for whom this deed is prepared.

[4] Not all of these definitions may be necessary, depending on the words defined in the Partnership Agreement of the firm for whom this Deed is prepared.

	any other future Partners for the time being
'Property'	the property described in the Schedule P vested in the Trustees by the documents set out in Schedule P
'Trustees'	the Partners whose names are set out in Part 2 of Schedule X and other Trustees for the time being hereof

1.2 Headings to Clauses and Schedules are for ease of reference only and shall be of no effect in construing the provisions of this Agreement

1.3 Where the context so admits:

 1.3.1 words importing the singular number shall include the plural and words importing the plural number shall include the singular

 1.3.2 references to statutes or to sections of statutes shall include any statutory modifications or re-enactments thereof for the time being in force

 [1.3.3 words defined in the Agreement shall where the context so admits have the same meaning in this Deed][5]

2. DECLARATION OF TRUST[6]

2.1 The Trustees declare that they hold the Property as trustees for and as part of the assets of the Firm in trust for the Partners in the shares in which they are from time to time entitled to share in capital of the Firm

2.2 The Partners hereby indemnify the Trustees against all claims for rent property taxes costs of repairs alterations or improvements and insurance relating to the Property and generally in respect of any obligations in respect of the Property[7]

2.3 Without prejudice to any statutory power if any Trustee shall cease to be a Partner in the Firm the other Partners may by deed remove him or her from the trusteeship hereof and by the same or any other deed or deeds may appoint one or more other persons (whether or not being the person or persons exercising the power) to be a trustee or trustees in place of the Partner so removed from the trusteeship and may by the same or another deed grant power of attorney to the person or persons so appointed in the name of the Partner so removed to execute any document necessary to vest the property comprised in the trust in the new trustees thereof[8]

---

[5] This subclause will not be necessary if no definitions from the Partnership Agreement are used. If possible, the same definitions should be used in both documents to avoid confusion.

[6] Care should be taken that this declaration does not constitute a breach of the terms of the lease.

[7] Although such an indemnity is implied, an express indemnity is better. As a result of the recession in the early 1990s a number of ex-partners have found themselves being sued on leases they signed for their firms many years ago, often without any formal documentation still in existence to prove their indemnity rights. Put a copy of this Deed with your will!

[8] Changes of title to property on partnership changes are often overlooked, and obtaining signatures later can be difficult, expensive and sometimes impossible particularly if a partner has not left on good terms.

3.   GENERAL

Each of the parties hereto agrees that he or she will execute and do all such deeds documents and things as may be necessary to carry this Deed into effect

SCHEDULE P

Description of the Property and Vesting Deed

The Property shortly known as [*description*] [transferred *or* let] to the Trustees by a [Transfer *or* Lease] dated the [. . .] day of [. . .] 199[. . .] made between (1) [*names*] and (2) [*Trustees*]

SCHEDULE X

Details of Partners Trustees and Execution

[This Deed is intended to be delivered on the date of this Deed
[. . .] is duly authorised to execute this Deed on behalf of the Partners][9]

Part 1
Partners

Name and Address	Signature as a Deed	Signature of Witness
[name (1)]	....	....
[name (2)]	....	....
[name (3)]	....	....
[name (4)]	....	....

---

[9] Alternative introductory wording is given. Some Partnership Agreements contain power of attorney for one partner to execute deeds on behalf of the firm. See Precedent 1: Standard Partnership Agreement, Clause 11.1 at p 31. In this case, Part 1 of the Schedule will need amendment to list only the names (apart from the signing partner) but not the signatures of the partners.

Part 2
Trustees

Name and Address	Signature as a Deed	Signature of Witness
[name (5)]	....	....
[name (6)]	....	....
[name (7)]	....	....
[name (8)]	....	....

PRECEDENT 14: ASSIGNMENT CLAUSES FOR INSERTION IN LEASES AND LICENCES TO ASSIGN TO PARTNERSHIPS[1]

1. This Clause applies whilst the term created by this Lease is vested in[2] any Partner or Partners for the time being in the Firm of [*firm name*] or any Firm which succeeds to the Practice of [*firm name*]

2. If any such Partner shall die or cease to be a Partner in [*firm name*]; and

    2.1   the Tenant shall apply to the Landlord under clause [*clause no*] of this Lease for Licence to Assign this Lease by substituting in his or her place another Partner or Partners in [*firm name*]; and

    2.2   the Landlord shall be satisfied that [*firm name*] will remain a respectable and responsible Tenant able to pay the rents hereby reserved and to perform and observe the covenants and conditions on the Tenant's part contained herein

then the Landlord shall consent (such consent not to be unreasonably withheld or delayed) to such Assignment and shall in a Deed permitting the Assignment (or in another contemporaneous Deed) release the estate of the deceased Partner or the former Partner (as the case may be) from all obligations under the terms of this Lease

---

[1] These suggested clauses are drawn from the tenant's perspective. Suitable amendments should be made if the clauses are inserted in a Licence to Assign to the firm rather than in the original Lease.

[2] There is no requirement for the firm to be trading from the premises.

PRECEDENT 15: TRUST CLAUSES[1] FOR INSERTION IN LEASES AND ASSIGNMENTS TO PARTNERSHIPS[2]

1.   DECLARATION OF TRUST[3]

1.1   In this Clause the following expressions shall where the context so admits have the following meanings

        'Firm'   the Firm of [*trade or business*] carried on under the name or style of [*firm name*] or any Firm which succeeds to its Practice

        'Trustees'   the said [*names of Partners taking lease*] or other the trustees for the time being hereof

1.2   The Trustees declare that they hold the Demised Premises as Trustees for and as part of the assets of the Firm in trust for the Partners in the Firm in the shares in which they are from time to time entitled to share in [capital *or* profits] of the Firm

1.3   Without prejudice to any statutory power if any Trustee shall cease to be a Partner in the Firm (and without prejudice to the provisions of Clause [*clause no*] of this Lease)[4] the other Partners may by deed remove him or her from the trusteeship hereof and by the same or any other deed or deeds may appoint one or more other persons (whether or not being the person or persons exercising the power) to be a Trustee or Trustees in place of the Partner so removed from the Trusteeship and may by the same or another deed grant power of attorney to the person or persons so appointed in the name of the Partner so removed to execute any document necessary to vest the property comprised in the Trust in the new Trustees thereof[5]

---

[1]   These clauses are not necessary if the Partnership Agreement contains Clauses 5.2 to 5.4 in Precedent 1: Standard Partnership Agreement.

[2]   It is preferable to keep Declarations of Trust in separate documents rather than in the Transfer or Lease – off the title. This is particularly the case with registered land where the Land Registry keep the original transfer. A separate form of Trust Deed is included as Precedent 13: Trust Deed for Partnership Property. Ideally, land should be vested in two companies as trustees and agents for the firm. Such documentation is outside the scope of this book.

[3]   Care should be taken that this declaration does not constitute a breach of the terms of the Lease.

[4]   Here refer to any provisions in the Lease or Licence to Assign requiring landlord's licence for an assignment. See Precedent 14: Assignment Clauses at p 201 for an example of special assignment provisions for partners.

[5]   Changes of title to property on partnership changes are often overlooked, and obtaining signatures later can be difficult, expensive and sometimes impossible particularly if a partner has not left on good terms. Omit this clause if there is already such a provision in the Partnership Agreement.

APPENDIX

Partnership Act 1890

(53 & 54 Vict c 39)

ARRANGEMENT OF SECTIONS

Nature of partnership

An Act to declare and amend the Law of Partnership [14 August 1890]

Nature of partnership

1 Definition of partnership

(1) Partnership is the relation which subsists between persons carrying on a business in common with a view of profit.

(2) But the relation between members of any company or association which is—

(*a*) Registered as a Company under the Companies Act 1862 or any other Act of Parliament for the time being in force and relating to the registration of joint stock companies; or

(*b*) Formed or incorporated by or in pursuance of any other Act of Parliament or letters patent, or Royal Charter; or

(*c*) A company engaged in working mines within and subject to the jurisdiction of the Stannaries:

is not a partnership within the meaning of this Act.

2 Rules for determining existence of partnership

In determining whether a partnership does or does not exist, regard shall be had to the following rules:

(1) Joint tenancy, tenancy in common, joint property, common property, or part ownership does not of itself create a partnership as to anything so held or owned, whether the tenants or owners do or do not share any profits made by the use thereof.

(2) The sharing of gross returns does not of itself create a partnership, whether the persons sharing such returns have or have not a joint or common right or interest in any property from which or from the use of which the returns are derived.

(3) The receipt by a person of a share of the profits of a business is *prima facie* evidence that he is a partner in the business, but receipt of such a share, or of a payment contingent on or

varying with the profits of a business, does not of itself make him a partner in the business; and in particular—

(a) The receipt by a person of a debt or other liquidated amount by instalments or otherwise out of the accruing profits of a business does not of itself make him a partner in the business or liable as such:

(b) A contract for the remuneration of a servant or agent of a person engaged in a business by a share of the profits of the business does not of itself make the servant or agent a partner in the business or liable as such:

(c) A person being the widow or child of a deceased partner, and receiving by way of annuity a portion of the profits made in the business in which the deceased person was a partner, is not by reason only of such receipt a partner in the business or liable as such:

(d) The advance of money by way of loan to a person engaged or about to engage in any business on a contract with that person that the lender shall receive a rate of interest varying with the profits, or shall receive a share of the profits arising from carrying on the business, does not of itself make the lender a partner with the person or persons carrying on the business or liable as such. Provided that the contract is in writing, and signed by or on behalf of all the parties thereto:

(e) A person receiving by way of annuity or otherwise a portion of the profits of a business in consideration of the sale by him of the goodwill of the business is not by reason only of such receipt a partner in the business or liable as such.

3 Postponement of rights of person lending or selling in consideration of share of profits in case of insolvency

In the event of any person to whom money has been advanced by way of loan upon such a contract as is mentioned in the last foregoing section, or of any buyer of a goodwill in consideration of a share of the profits of the business, being adjudged a bankrupt, entering into an arrangement to pay his creditors less than [100p] in the pound, or dying in insolvent circumstances, the lender of the loan shall not be entitled to recover anything in respect of his loan, and the seller of the goodwill shall not be entitled to recover anything in respect of the share of profits contracted for, until the claims of the other creditors of the borrower or buyer for valuable consideration in money or money's worth have been satisfied.

4 Meaning of firm

(1) Persons who have entered into partnership with one another are for the purposes of this Act called collectively a firm, and the name under which their business is carried on is called the firm-name.

(2) *(Applies in Scotland only.)*

Relations of partners to persons dealing with them

5 Power of partner to bind the firm

Every partner is an agent of the firm and his other partners for the purpose of the business of the partnership; and the acts of every partner who does any act for carrying on in the usual way business of the kind carried on by the firm of which he is a member bind the firm and his partners, unless the partner so acting has in fact no authority to act for the firm in the particular matter, and the person with whom he is dealing either knows that he has no authority, or does not know or believe him to be a partner.

6 Partners bound by acts on behalf of firm

An act or instrument relating to the business of the firm done or executed in the firm-name, or in any other manner showing an intention to bind the firm, by any person thereto authorised, whether a partner or not, is binding on the firm and all the partners.

Provided that this section shall not affect any general rule of law relating to the execution of deeds or negotiable instruments.

7 Partner using credit of firm for private purposes

Where one partner pledges the credit of the firm for a purpose apparently not connected with the firm's ordinary course of business, the firm is not bound, unless he is in fact specially authorised by the other partners; but this section does not affect any personal liability incurred by an individual partner.

8 Effect of notice that firm will not be bound by acts of partner

If it has been agreed between the partners that any restriction shall be placed on the power of any one or more of them to bind the firm, no act done in contravention of the agreement is binding on the firm with respect to persons having notice of the agreement.

9 Liability of partners

Every partner in a firm is liable jointly with the other partners, and in Scotland severally also, for all debts and obligations of the firm incurred while he is a parnter; and after his death his estate is also severally liable in a due course of administration for such debts and obligations, so far as they remain unsatisfied, but subject in England or Ireland to the prior payment of his separate debts.

10 Liability of the firm for wrongs

Where, by any wrongful act or omission of any partner acting in the ordinary course of the business of the firm, or with the authority of his co-partners, loss or injury is caused to any person not being a partner in the firm, or any penalty is incurred, the firm is liable therefor to the same extent as the partner so acting or omitting to act.

11 Misapplication of money or property received for or in custody of the firm

In the following cases; namely—

(a) Where one partner acting within the scope of his apparent authority receives the money or property of a third person and misapplies it; and
(b) Where a firm in the course of its business receives money or property of a third person, and the money or property so received is misapplied by one or more of the partners while it is in the custody of the firm;

the firm is liable to make good the loss.

12 Liability for wrongs joint and several

Every partner is liable jointly with his co-partners and also severally for everything for which the firm while he is a partner therein becomes liable under either of the two last preceding sections.

13 Improper employment of trust-property for partnership purposes

If a partner, being a trustee, improperly employs trust-property in the business or on the account of the partnership, no other partner is liable for the trust property to the persons beneficially interested therein:

Provided as follows:—

(1) This section shall not affect any liability incurred by any partner by reason of his having notice of a breach of trust; and

(2) Nothing in this section shall prevent trust money from being followed and recovered from the firm if still in its possession or under its control.

14 Persons liable by 'holding out'

(1) Every one who by words spoken or written or by conduct represents himself, or who knowingly suffers himself to be represented, as a partner in a particular firm, is liable as a partner to any one who has on the faith of any such representation given credit to the firm, whether the representation has or has not been made or communicated to the person so giving credit by or with the knowledge of the apparent partner making the representation or suffering it to be made.

(2) Provided that where after a partner's death the partnership business is continued in the old firm's name, the continued use of that name or of the deceased partner's name as part thereof shall not of itself make his executors or administrators estate or effects liable for any partnership debts contracted after his death.

15 Admissions and representations of partners

An admission or representation made by any partner concerning the partnership affairs, and in the ordinary course of its business, is evidence against the firm.

16 Notice to acting partner to be notice to the firm

Notice to any partner who habitually acts in the partnership business of any matter relating to partnership affairs operates as notice to the firm, except in the case of a fraud on the firm committed by or with the consent of that partner.

17 Liabilities of incoming and outgoing partners

(1) A person who is admitted as a partner into an existing firm does not thereby become liable to the creditors of the firm for anything done before he became a partner.

(2) A partner who retires from a firm does not thereby cease to be liable for partnership debts or obligations incurred before his retirement.

(3) A retiring partner may be discharged from any existing liabilities, by an agreement to that effect between himself and the members of the firm as newly constituted and the creditors, and this agreement may be either expressed or inferred as a fact from the course of dealing between the creditors and the firm as newly constituted.

18 Revocation of continuing guaranty by change in firm

A continuing guaranty or cautionary obligation given either to a firm or to a third person in respect of the transactions of a firm is, in the absence of agreement to the contrary, revoked as to future transactions by any change in the constitution of the firm to which, or of the firm in respect of the transactions of which, the guaranty or obligation was given.

Relations of partners to one another

19 Variation by consent of terms of partnership

The mutual rights and duties of partners, whether ascertained by agreement or defined by this Act, may be varied by the consent of all the partners, and such consent may be either express or inferred from a course of dealing.

20 Partnership property

(1) All property and rights and interests in property originally brought into the partnership stock or acquired, whether by purchase or otherwise, on account of the firm, or for the purposes and in the course of the partnership business, are called in this Act partnership property, and must be held and applied by the partners exclusively for the purposes of the partnership and in accordance with the partnership agreement.

(2) Provided that the legal estate or interest in any land, or in Scotland the title to and interest in any heritable estate, which belongs to the partnership shall devolve according to the nature and tenure thereof, and the general rules of law thereto applicable, but in trust, so far as necessary, for the persons beneficially interested in the land under this section.

(3) Where co-owners of an estate or interest in any land, or in Scotland of any heritable estate, not being itself partnership property, are partners as to profits made by the use of that land or estate, and purchase other land or estate out of the profits to be used in like manner, the land or estate so purchased belongs to them, in the absence of an agreement to the contrary, not as partners, but as co-owners for the same respective estates and interests as are held by them in the land or estate first mentioned at the date of the purchase.

21 Property bought with partnership money

Unless the contrary intention appears, property bought with money belonging to the firm is deemed to have been bought on account of the firm.

22 Conversion into personal estate of land held as partnership property

Where land or any heritable interest therein has become partnership property, it shall, unless the contrary intention appears, be treated as between the partners (including the representatives of a deceased partner), and also as between the heirs of a deceased partner and his executors or administrators, as personal or moveable and not real or heritable estate.

23 Procedure against partnership property for a partner's separate judgment debt

(1) A writ of execution shall not issue against any partnership property except on a judgment against the firm.

(2) The High Court, or a judge thereof, or a county court, may, on the application by summons of any judgment creditor of a partner, make an order charging that partner's interest in the partnership property and profits with payment of the amount of the judgment debt and interest thereon, and may by the same or a subsequent order appoint a receiver of that partner's share of profits (whether already declared or accruing), and of any other money which may be coming to him in respect of the partnership, and direct all accounts and inquiries, and give all other orders and directions which might have been directed or given if the charge had been made in favour of the judgment creditor by the partner, or which the circumstances of the case may require.

(3) The other partner or partners shall be at liberty at any time to redeem the interest charged, or in case of a sale being directed, to purchase the same.

(4) This section shall apply in the case of a cost-book company as if the company were a partnership within the meaning of this Act.

(5) This section shall not apply to Scotland.

24 Rules as to interests and duties of partners subject to special agreement

The interests of partners in the partnership property and their rights and duties in relation to the partnership shall be determined, subject to any agreement express or implied between the partners, by the following rules:—

    (1) All the partners are entitled to share equally in the capital and profits of the business, and must contribute equally towards the losses whether of capital or otherwise sustained by the firm.

    (2) The firm must indemnify every partner in respect of payments made and personal liabilities incurred by him—

        (*a*) In the ordinary and proper conduct of the business of the firm; or,

        (*b*) In or about anything necessarily done for the preservation of the business or property of the firm.

    (3) A partner making, for the purpose of the partnership, any actual payment or advance beyond the amount of capital which he has agreed to subscribe, is entitled to interest at the rate of five per cent. per annum from the date of the payment or advance.

    (4) A partner is not entitled, before the ascertainment of profits, to interest on the capital subscribed by him.

    (5) Every partner may take part in the management of the partnership business.

    (6) No partner shall be entitled to remuneration for acting in the partnership business.

    (7) No person may be introduced as a partner without the consent of all existing partners.

    (8) Any difference arising as to ordinary matters connected with the partnership business may be decided by a majority of the partners, but no change may be made in the nature of the partnership business without the consent of all existing partners.

    (9) The partnership books are to be kept at the place of business of the partnership (or the principal place, if there is more than one), and every partner may, when he thinks fit, have access to and inspect and copy any of them.

25 Expulsion of partner

No majority of the partners can expel any partner unless a power to do so has been conferred by express agreement between the partners.

26 Retirement from partnership at will

(1) Where no fixed term has been agreed upon for the duration of the partnership, any partner may determine the partnership at any time on giving notice of his intention so to do to all the other partners.

(2) Where the partnership has originally been constituted by deed, a notice in writing, signed by the partner giving it, shall be sufficient for this purpose.

27 Where partnership for term is continued over, continuance on old terms presumed

(1) Where a partnership entered into for a fixed term is continued after the term has expired, and without any express new agreement, the rights and duties of the partners remain the same

as they were at the expiration of the term, so far as is consistent with the incidents of a partnership at will.

(2) A continuance of the business by the partners or such of them as habitually acted therein during the term, without any settlement or liquidation of the partnership affairs, is presumed to be a continuance of the partnership.

28 Duty of partners to render accounts, etc

Partners are bound to render true accounts and full information of all things affecting the partnership to any partner or his legal representatives.

29 Accountability of partners for private profits

(1) Every partner must account to the firm for any benefit derived by him without the cosnent of the other partners from any transaction concerning the partnership, or from any use by him of the partnership property name or business connexion.

(2) This section applies also to transactions undertaken after a partnership has been dissolved by the death of a partner, and before the affairs thereof have been completely wound up, either by any surviving partner or by the representatives of the deceased partner.

30 Duty of partner not to compete with firm

If a partner, without the consent of the other partners, carries on any business of the same nature as and competing with that of the firm, he must account for and pay over to the firm all profits made by him in that business.

31 Rights of assignee of share in partnership

(1) An assignment by any partner of his share in the partnership, either absolute or by way of mortgage or redeemable charge, does not, as against the other partners, entitle the assignee, during the continuance of the partnership, to interfere in the management or administration of the partnership business or affairs, or to require any accounts of the partnership transactions, or to inspect the partnership books, but entitles the assignee only to receive the share of profits to which the assigning partner would otherwise be entitled, and the assignee must accept the account of profits agreed to by the partners.

(2) In case of a dissolution of the partnership, whether as respects all the partners or as respects the assigning partner, the assignee is entitled to receive the share of the partnership assets to which the assigning partner is entitled as between himself and the other partners, and, for the purpose of ascertaining that share, to an account as from the date of the dissolution.

Dissolution of partnership and its consequences

32 Dissolution by expiration or notice

Subject to any agreement between the partners, a partnership is dissolved—

    (*a*) If entered into for a fixed term, by the expiration of that term:
    (*b*) If entered into for a single adventure or undertaking, by the termination of that adventure or undertaking:
    (*c*) If entered into for an undefined time, by any partner giving notice to the other or others of his intention to dissolve the partnership.

In the last-mentioned case the partnership is dissolved as from the date mentioned in the notice as the date of dissolution, or, if no date is so mentioned, as from the date of the communication of the notice.

33 Dissolution by bankruptcy, death or charge

(1) Subject to any agreement between the partners, every partnership is dissolved as regards all the partners by the death or bankruptcy of any partner.

(2) A partnership may, at the option of the other partners, be dissolved if any partner suffers his share of the partnership property to be charged under this Act for his separate debt.

34 Dissolution by illegality of partnership

A partnership is in every case dissolved by the happening of any event which makes it unlawful for the business of the firm to be carried on or for the members of the firm to carry it on in partnership.

35 Dissolution by the Court

On application by a partner the Court may decree a dissolution of the partnership in any of the following cases:

  (*a*) . . .
  (*b*) When a partner, other than the partner suing, becomes in any other way permanently incapable of performing his part of the partnership contract:
  (*c*) When a partner, other than the partner suing, has been guilty of such conduct as, in the opinion of the Court, regard being had to the nature of the business, is calculated to prejudicially affect the carrying on of the business:
  (*d*) When a partner, other than the partner suing, wilfully or persistently commits a breach of the partnership agreement, or otherwise so conducts himself in matters relating to the partnership business that it is not reasonably practicable for the other partner or partners to carry on the business in partnership with him:
  (*e*) When the business of the partnership can only be carried on at a loss:
  (*f*) Whenever in any case circumstances have arisen which, in the opinion of the Court, render it just and equitable that the partnership be dissolved.

36 Rights of persons dealing with firm against apparent members of firm

(1) Where a person deals with a firm after a change in its constitution he is entitled to treat all apparent members of the old firm as still being members of the firm until he has notice of the change.

(2) An advertisement in the London Gazette as to a firm whose principal place of business is in England or Wales, in the Edinburgh Gazette as to a firm whose principal place of business is in Scotland, and in the Dublin Gazette as to a firm whose principal place of business is in Ireland, shall be notice as to persons who had no dealings with the firm before the date of the dissolution or change so advertised.

(3) The estate of a partner who dies, or who becomes bankrupt, or of a partner who, not having been known to the person dealing with the firm to be a partner, retires from the firm, is not liable for partnership debts contracted after the date of the death, bankruptcy, or retirement respectively.

37 Right of partners to notify dissolution

On the dissolution of a partnership or retirement of a partner any partner may publicly notify the same, and may require the other partner or partners to concur for that purpose in all necessary or proper acts, if any, which cannot be done without his or their concurrence.

38 Continuing authority of partners for purposes of winding up

After the dissolution of a partnership the authority of each partner to bind the firm, and the other rights and obligations of the partners, continue notwithstanding the dissolution so far as may be necessary to wind up the affairs of the partnership, and to complete transactions begun but unfinished at the time of the dissolution, but not otherwise.

Provided that the firm is in no case bound by the acts of a partner who has become bankrupt; but this proviso does not affect the liability of any person who has after the bankruptcy represented himself or knowingly suffered himself to be represented as a partner of the bankrupt.

39 Rights of partners as to application of partnership property

On the dissolution of a partnership every partner is entitled, as against the other partners in the firm, and all persons claiming through them in respect of their interests as partners, to have the property of the partnership applied in payment of the debts and liabilities of the firm, and to have the surplus assets after such payment applied in payment of what may be due to the partners respectively after deducting what may be due from them as partners to the firm; and for that purpose any partner or his representatives may on the termination of the partnership apply to the Court to wind up the business and affairs of the firm.

40 Apportionment of premium where partnership prematurely dissolved

Where one partner has paid a premium to another on entering into a partnership for a fixed term, and the partnership is dissolved before the expiration of that term otherwise than by the death of a partner, the Court may order the repayment of the premium, or of such part thereof as it thinks just, having regard to the terms of the partnership contract and to the length of time during which the partnership has continued; unless

(a) the dissolution is, in the judgment of the Court, wholly or chiefly due to the misconduct of the partner who paid the premium; or

(b) the partnership has been dissolved by an agreement containing no provision for a return of any part of the premium.

41 Rights where partnership dissolved for fraud or misrepresentation

Where a partnership contract is rescinded on the ground of the fraud or misrepresentation of one of the parties thereto, the party entitled to rescind is, without prejudice to any other right, entitled—

(a) to a lien on, or right of retention of, the surplus of the partnership assets, after satisfying the partnership liabilities, for any sum of money paid by him for the purchase of a share in the partnership and for any capital contributed by him, and is

(b) to stand in the place of the creditors of the firm for any payments made by him in respect of the partnership liabilities, and

(c) to be indemnified by the person guilty of the fraud or making the representation against all the debts and liabilities of the firm.

42 Right of outgoing partner in certain cases to share profits made after dissolution

(1) Where any member of a firm has died or otherwise ceased to be a partner, and the surviving or continuing partners carry on the business of the firm with its capital or assets without any final settlement of accounts as between the firm and the outgoing partner or his

estate, then, in the absence of any agreement to the contrary, the outgoing partner or his estate is entitled at the option of himself or his representatives to such share of the profits made since the dissolution as the Court may find to be attributable to the use of his share of the partnership assets, or to interest at the rate of five per cent. per annum on the amount of his share of the partnership assets.

(2) Provided that where by the partnership contract an option is given to surviving or continuing partners to purchase the interest of a deceased or outgoing partner, and that option is duly exercised, the estate of the deceased partner, or the outgoing partner or his estate, as the case may be, is not entitled to any further or other share of profits; but if any partner assuming to act in exercise of the option does not in all material respects comply with the terms thereof, he is liable to account under the foregoing provisions of this section.

43 Retiring or deceased partner's share to be a debt

Subject to any agreement between the partners, the amount due from surviving or continuing partners to an outgoing partner or the representatives of a deceased partner in respect of the outgoing or deceased partner's share is a debt accruing at the date of the dissolution or death.

44 Rule for distribution of assets on final settlement of accounts

In settling accounts between the partners after a dissolution of partnership, the following rules shall, subject to any agreement, be observed:

(a) Losses, including losses and deficiencies of capital, shall be paid first out of profits, next out of capital, and lastly, if necessary, by the partners individually in the proportion in which they were entitled to share profits:

(b) The assets of the firm including the sums, if any, contributed by the partners to make up losses or deficiencies of capital, shall be applied in the following manner and order:

1. In paying the debts and liabilities of the firm to persons who are not partners therein:
2. In paying to each partner rateably what is due from the firm to him for advances as distinguished from capital:
3. In paying to each partner rateably what is due from the firm to him in respect of capital:
4. The ultimate residue, if any, shall be divided among the partners in the proportion in which profits are divisible.

Supplemental

45 Definitions of 'court' and 'business'

In this Act, unless the contrary intention appears,—

The expression 'court' includes every court and judge having jurisdiction in the case:

The expression 'business' includes every trade, occupation, or profession.

46 Saving for rules of equity and common law

The rules of equity and of common law applicable to partnership shall continue in force except so far as they are inconsistent with the express provisions of this Act.

Sex Discrimination Act 1975

Discrimination by other bodies

11 Partnerships

(1) It is unlawful for a firm, in relation to a position as partner in the firm, to discriminate against a woman—

    (*a*) in the arrangements they make for the purpose of determining who should be offered that position, or

    (*b*) in the terms on which they offer her that position, or

    (*c*) by refusing or deliberately omitting to offer her that position, or

    (*d*) in a case where the woman already holds that position—

        (i) in the way they afford her access to any benefits, facilities or services, or by refusing or deliberately omitting to afford her access to them, or

        (ii) by expelling her from that position, or subjecting her to any other detriment.

(2) Subsection (1) shall apply in relation to persons proposing to form themselves into a partnership as it applies in relation to a firm.

(3) Subsection (1)(*a*) and (*c*) do not apply to a position as partner where, if it were employment, being a man would be a genuine occupational qualification for the job.

(4) Subsection (1)(*b*) and (*d*) do not apply to provision made in relation to death or retirement except in so far as, in their application to provision made in relation to retirement, they render it unlawful for a firm to discriminate against a woman—

    (*a*) in such of the terms on which they offer her a position as partner as provide for her expulsion from that position; or

    (*b*) by expelling her from a position as partner or subjecting her to any detriment which results in her expulsion from such a position.

(5) In the case of a limited partnership references in subsection (1) to a partner shall be construed as references to a general partner as defined in section 3 of the Limited Partnership Act 1907.

Race Relations Act 1976

Discrimination by other bodies

10 Partnerships

(1) It is unlawful for a firm consisting of six or more partners, in relation to a position as partner in the firm, to discriminate against a person—

(a) in the arrangements they make for the purpose of determining who should be offered that position; or

(b) in the terms on which they offer him that position; or

(c) by refusing or deliberately omitting to offer him that position; or

(d) in a case where the person already holds that position—

(i) in the way they afford him access to any benefits, facilities or services, or by refusing or deliberately omitting to afford him access to them; or

(ii) by expelling him from that position, or subjecting him to any other detriment.

(2) Subsection (1) shall apply in relation to persons proposing to form themselves into a partnership as it applies in relation to a firm.

(3) Subsection (1)(a) and (c) do not apply to a position as partner where, if it were employment, being of a particular racial group would be a genuine occupational qualification for the job.

(4) In the case of a limited partnership references in this section to a partner shall be construed as references to a general partner as defined in section 3 of the Limited Partnerships Act 1907.

Business Names Act 1985

(1985 c 7)

ARRANGEMENT OF SECTIONS

An Act to consolidate certain enactments relating to the names under which persons may carry on business in Great Britain   [11 March 1985]

1 Persons subject to this Act

(1) This Act applies to any person who has a place of business in Great Britain and who carries on business in Great Britain under a name which—

(a) in the case of a partnership, does not consist of the surnames of all partners who are individuals and the corporate names of all partners who are bodies corporate without any addition other than an addition permitted by this Act;

(b) in the case of an individual, does not consist of his surname without any addition other than one so permitted;

(c) in the case of a company, being a company which is capable of being wound up under the Companies Act 1985, does not consist of its corporate name without any addition other than one so permitted.

(2) The following are permitted additions for the purposes of subsection (1)—

(a) in the case of a partnership, the forenames of individual partners or the initials of those forenames or, where two or more individual partners have the same surname, the addition of 's' at the end of that surname; or

(b) in the case of an individual, his forename or its initial;

(c) in any case, any addition merely indicating that the business is carried on in succession to a former owner of the business.

2 Prohibition of use of certain business names

(1) Subject to the following subsections, a person to whom this Act applies shall not, without the written approval of the Secretary of State, carry on business in Great Britain under a name which—

(a) would be likely to give the impression that the business is connected with Her Majesty's Government or with any local authority; or

(b) includes any word or expression for the time being specified in regulations made under this Act.

(2) Subsection (1) does not apply to the carrying on of a business by a person—

    (*a*) to whom the business has been transferred on or after 26th February 1982; and

    (*b*) who carries on the business under the name which was its lawful business name immediately before that transfer,

during the period of 12 months beginning with the date of that transfer.

(3) Subsection (1) does not apply to the carrying on of a business by a person who—

    (*a*) carried on that business immediately before 26th February 1982; and

    (*b*) continues to carry it on under the name which immediately before that date was its lawful business name.

(4) A person who contravenes subsection (1) is guilty of an offence.

3 Words and expressions requiring Secretary of State's approval

(1) The Secretary of State may by regulations—

    (*a*) specify words or expressions for the use of which as or as part of a business name his approval is required by section 2(1)(*b*); and

    (*b*) in relation to any such word or expression, specify a Government department or other body as the relevant body for purposes of the following subsection.

(2) Where a person to whom this Act applies proposes to carry on a business under a name which is or includes any such word or expression, and a Government department or other body is specified under subsection (1)(*b*) in relation to that word or expression, that person shall—

    (*a*) request (in writing) the relevant body to indicate whether (and if so why) it has any objections to the proposal; and

    (*b*) submit to the Secretary of State a statement that such a request has been made and a copy of any response received from the relevant body.

4 Disclosure required of persons using business names

(1) A person to whom this Act applies shall—

    (*a*) subject to subsection (3), state in legible characters on all business letters, written orders for goods or services to be supplied to the business, invoices and receipts issued in the course of the business and written demands for payment of debts arising in the course of the business—

        (i) in the case of a partnership, the name of each partner,

        (ii) in the case of an individual, his name,

        (iii) in the case of a company, its corporate name, and

        (iv) in relation to each person so named, an address in Great Britain at which service of any document relating in any way to the business will be effective; and

    (*b*) in any premises where the business is carried on and to which the customers of the business or suppliers of any goods or services to the business have access, display in a prominent position so that it may easily be read by such customers or suppliers a notice containing such names and addresses.

(2) A person to whom this Act applies shall secure that the names and addresses required by subsection (1)(*a*) to be stated on his business letters, or which would have been so required but for the subsection next following, are immediately given, by written notice to any person with whom anything is done or discussed in the course of the business and who asks for such names and addresses.

(3) Subsection (1)(*a*) does not apply in relation to any document issued by a partnership of more than 20 persons which maintains at its principal place of business a list of the names of all the partners if—

(*a*) none of the names of the partners appears in the document otherwise than in the test or as a signatory; and

(*b*) the document states in legible characters the address of the partnership's principal place of business and that the list of the partners' names is open to inspection at that place.

(4) Where a partnership maintains a list of the partners' names for purposes of subsection (3), any person may inspect the list during office hours.

(5) The Secretary of State may by regulations require notices under subsection (1)(*b*) or (2) to be displayed or given in a specified form.

(6) A person who without reasonable excuse contravenes subsection (1) or (2), or any regulations made under subsection (5), is guilty of an offence.

(7) Where an inspection required by a person in accordance with subsection (4) is refused, any partner of the partnership concerned who without reasonable excuse refused that inspection, or permitted it to be refused, is guilty of an offence.

5 Civil remedies for breach of s 4

(1) Any legal proceedings brought by a person to whom this Act applies to enforce a right arising out of a contract made in the course of a business in respect of which he was, at the time the contract was made, in breach of subsection (1) or (2) of section 4 shall be dismissed if the defendant (or, in Scotland, the defender) to the proceedings shows—

(*a*) that he has a claim against the plaintiff (pursuer) arising out of that contract which he has been unable to pursue by reason of the latter's breach of section 4(1) or (2), or

(*b*) that he has suffered some financial loss in connection with the contract by reason of the plaintiff's (pursuer's) breach of section 4(1) or (2),

unless the court before which the proceedings are brought is satisfied that it is just and equitable to permit the proceedings to continue.

(2) This section is without prejudice to the right of any person to enforce such rights as he may have against another person in any proceedings brought by that person.

6 Regulations

(1) Regulations under this Act shall be made by statutory instrument and may contain such transitional provisions and savings as the Secretary of State thinks appropriate, and may make different provision for different cases or classes of case.

(2) In the case of regulations made under section 3, the statutory instrument containing them shall be laid before Parliament after the regulations are made and shall cease to have effect at the end of the period of 28 days beginning with the day on which they were made (but without prejudice to anything previously done by virtue of them or to the making of new regulations) unless during that period they are approved by a resolution of each House of Parliament.

In reckoning this period of 28 days, no account is to be taken of any time during which Parliament is dissolved or prorogued, or during which both Houses are adjourned for more than 4 days.

(3) In the case of regulations made under section 4, the statutory instrument containing them is subject to annulment in pursuance of a resolution of either House of Parliament.

7 Offences

(1) Offences under this Act are punishable on summary conviction.

(2) A person guilty of an offence under this Act is liable to a fine not exceeding one-fifth of the statutory maximum.

(3) If after a person has been convicted summarily of an offence under section 2 or 4(6) the original contravention is continued, he is liable on a second or subsequent summary conviction of the offence to a fine not exceeding one-fiftieth of the statutory maximum for each day on which the contravention is continued (instead of to the penalty which may be imposed on the first conviction of the offence).

(4) Where an offence under section 2 or 4(6) or (7) committed by a body corporate is proved to have been committed with the consent or connivance of, or to be attributable to any neglect on the part of, any director, manager, secretary or other similar officer of the body corporate, or any person who was purporting to act in any such capacity, he as well as the body corporate is guilty of the offence and liable to be proceeded against and punished accordingly.

(5) Where the affairs of a body corporate are managed by its members, subsection (4) applies in relation to the acts and defaults of a member in connection with his functions of management as if he were a director of the body corporate.

(6) For purposes of the following provisions of the Companies Act 1985—

   (*a*) section 731 (summary proceedings under the Companies Acts), and
   (*b*) section 732(3) (legal professional privilege),

this Act is to be treated as included in those Acts.

8 Interpretation

(1) The following definitions apply for purposes of this Act—

   'business' includes a profession;
   'initial' includes any recognised abbreviation of a name;
   'lawful business name', in relation to a business, means a name under which the business
        was carried on without contravening section 2(1) of this Act or section 2 of the
        Registration of Business Names Act 1916;
   'local authority' means any local authority within the meaning of the Local Govern-
        ment Act 1972 or the Local Government (Scotland) Act 1973, the Common
        Council of the City of London or the Council of the Isles of Scilly;
   'partnership' includes a foreign partnership;
   'statutory maximum' means—

        (*a*) in England and Wales the prescribed sum under section 32 of the Magistrates'
             Courts Act 1980, and
        (*b*) in Scotland, the prescribed sum under section 289B of the Criminal
             Procedure (Scotland) Act 1975;

   and 'surname', in relation to a peer or person usually known by a British title different
        from his surname, means the title by which he is known.

(2) Any expression used in this Act and also in the Companies Act 1985 has the same meaning in this Act as in that.

9 Northern Ireland

This Act does not extend to Northern Ireland.

10 Commencement

This Act comes into force on 1st July 1985.

11 Citation

This Act may be cited as the Business Names Act 1985.

Companies Act 1985

PART XXV
MISCELLANEOUS AND SUPPLEMENTARY PROVISIONS

716 Prohibition of partnerships with more than 20 members

(1) No company, association or partnership consisting of more than 20 persons shall be formed for the purpose of carrying on any business that has for its object the acquisition of gain by the company, association or partnership, or by its individual members, unless it is registered as a company under this Act, or is formed in pursuance of some other Act of Parliament, or of letters patent.

(2) However, this does not prohibit the formation—

(a) for the purpose of carrying on practice as solicitors, of a partnership consisting of persons each of whom is a solicitor;

(b) for the purpose of carrying on practice as accountants, of a partnership which is eligible for appointment as a company auditor under section 25 of the Companies Act 1989;

(c) for the purpose of carrying on business as members of a recognised stock exchange, of a partnership consisting of persons each of whom is a member of that stock exchange;

(d) for any purpose prescribed by regulations (which may include a purpose mentioned above), of a partnership of a description so prescribed.

(3) In subsection (2)(a) 'solicitor'—

(a) in relation to England and Wales, means solicitor of the Supreme Court, and

(b) in relation to Scotland, means a person enrolled or deemed enrolled as a solicitor in pursuance of the Solicitors (Scotland) Act 1980.

(4) In subsection (2)(c) 'recognised stock exchange' means—

(a) The International Stock Exchange of the United Kingdom and the Republic of Ireland Limited, and

(b) any other stock exchange for the time being recognised for the purposes of this section by the Secretary of State by order made by statutory instrument.

(5) Subsection (1) does not apply in relation to any body of persons for the time being approved for the purposes of the Marine and Aviation Insurance (War Risks) Act 1952 by the Secretary of State, being a body the objects of which are or include the carrying on of business by way of the re-insurance of risks which may be re-insured under any agreement for the purpose mentioned in section 1(1)(b) of that Act.

Income and Corporation Taxes Act 1988

CHAPTER VII
PARTNERSHIPS AND SUCCESSIONS

General

111 Partnership assessments to income tax

Where a trade or profession is carried on by two or more persons jointly, income tax in respect thereof shall be computed and stated jointly, and in one sum, and shall be separate and distinct from any other tax chargeable on those persons or any of them, and a joint assessment shall be made in the partnership name.

111 Treatment of partnerships[1]

(1) Where a trade or profession is carried on by two or more persons in partnership, the partnership shall not, unless the contrary intention appears, be treated for the purposes of the Tax Acts as an entity which is separate and distinct from those persons.

(2) So long as a trade or profession ('the actual trade or profession') is carried on by persons in partnership, and each of those persons is chargeable to income tax, the profits or gains or losses arising from the trade or profession shall be computed for the purposes of income tax in like manner as if the partnership were an individual.

(3) A person's share in the profits or gains or losses of the partnership which for any period are computed in accordance with subsection (2) above shall be determined according to the interests of the partners during that period; and income tax shall be chargeable or, as the case may require, loss relief may be claimed as if—

    (*a*) that share derived from a trade or profession ('the deemed trade or profession') carried on by the person alone;

    (*b*) the deemed trade or profession was set up and commenced by him at the time when he became a partner or, where the actual trade or profession was previously carried on by him alone, the time when the actual trade was set up and commenced; and

    (*c*) the deemed trade or profession is permanently discontinued by him at the time when he ceases to be a partner or, where the actual trade or profession is subsequently carried on by him alone, the time when the actual trade or profession is permanently discontinued.

(4) Where—

    (*a*) subsections (2) and (3) above apply in relation to the profits or gains or losses of a trade or profession carried on by persons in partnership, and

    (*b*) other income accrues to those persons by virtue of their being partners,

that other income shall be chargeable to tax by reference to the same periods as if it were profits or gains arising from the trade or profession.

(5) Subsections (1) to (3) above apply, with the necessary modifications, in relation to a business as they apply in relation to a trade.

    [1]   This new version of s 111 has effect:
    (1) As respects partnerships commenced after 5 April 1994 which are not controlled abroad, from the year 1994–95.
    (2) As respects partnerships commenced before 6 April 1994 which are not controlled abroad, from the year 1997–98.

Value Added Tax Act 1994

45 Partnerships

(1) The registration under this Act of persons—

(a) carrying on a business in partnership, or

(b) carrying on in partnership any other activities in the course or furtherance of which they acquire goods from other member States,

may be in the name of the firm; and no account shall be taken, in determining for any purpose of this Act whether goods or services are supplied to or by such persons or are acquired by such persons from another member State, of any change in the partnership.

(2) Without prejudice to section 36 of the Partnership Act 1890 (rights of persons dealing with firm against apparent members of firm), until the date on which a change in the partnership is notified to the Commissioners a person who has ceased to be a member of a partnership shall be regarded as continuing to be a partner for the purposes of this Act and, in particular, for the purpose of any liability for VAT on the supply of goods or services by the partnership or on the acquisition of goods by the partnership from another member State.

(3) Where a person ceases to be a member of a partnership during a prescribed accounting period (or is treated as so doing by virtue of subsection (2) above) any notice, whether of assessment or otherwise, which is served on the partnership and relates to, or to any matter arising in, that period or any earlier period during the whole or part of which he was a member of the partnership shall be treated as served also on him.

(4) Without prejudice to section 16 of the Partnership Act 1890 (notice to acting partner to be notice to the firm) any notice, whether of assessment or otherwise, which is addressed to a partnership by the name in which it is registered by virtue of subsection (1) above and is served in accordance with this Act shall be treated for the purposes of this Act as served on the partnership and, accordingly, where subsection (3) above applies, as served also on the former partner.

(5) Subsections (1) and (3) above shall not affect the extent to which, under section 9 of the Partnership Act 1890, a partner is liable for VAT owed by the firm; but where a person is a partner in a firm during part only of a prescribed accounting period, his liability for VAT on the supply by the firm of goods or services during that accounting period or on the acquisition during that period by the firm of any goods from another member State shall be such proportion of the firm's liability as may be just.

INDEX

References are to page numbers